Slow Down to Speed Up

Slow Down to Speed Up

*Lead, Succeed, and Thrive
in a 24/7 World*

Liz Bywater, PhD

BUSINESS EXPERT PRESS

First published in 2018 by
Business Expert Press, LLC
222 East 46th Street, New York, NY 10017
www.businessexpertpress.com

ISBN-13: 978-1-94744-155-2 (paperback)
ISBN-13: 978-1-94744-156-9 (e-book)

Business Expert Press Human Resource Management and Organizational Behavior Collection

Collection ISSN: 1946-5637 (print)
Collection ISSN: 1946-5645 (electronic)

Cover and interior design by S4Carlisle Publishing Services
Private Ltd., Chennai, India

First edition: 2018

10 9 8 7 6 5 4 3 2 1

Printed in the United States of America.

Advance Quotes for
Slow Down to Speed Up

"Liz provides an in-depth look at something we all struggle with—finding the balance. These real-life examples provide insight into some innovative new thinking around the pragmatism of finding high-impact results in the middle of changing priorities and the constant search for overall effectiveness."

David and Esperanza Neu
Founders, Neu Center for Supportive Medicine and Cancer Survivorship

"*Slowing Down to Speed Up* sounds like common sense. Why then do so many of us fail to execute on such a basic principle? Perhaps it is because we lack the tools that are necessary to make the process effective. Unlike many leadership books that utilize analogies and parables, Liz Bywater, Ph.D., provides guidance built on real-world examples, and incorporates instructive tools derived from her many years working as an executive consultant. If looking for a quick fix then this book is not for you. Because although Bywater's work is a quick read, mastering the principle requires you to not just read, but reflect, engage, and slow down to get the most out of her advice."

Rob Wright
Chief Editor, Life Science Leader magazine

"I have worked with Liz and greatly benefitted from her advice and the tools she has developed over a long career of advising executives. Everything Liz says seems so logical, you find yourself saying *That makes sense!* She creates a very easy system to get you to reflect, reprioritize, and create a vision for personal and career success. The stopping to accelerate, as Liz says, to *speed up*, is true in my own career. I love having these tools all in one book.

Having the toolkit to put your thoughts into action is invaluable."

Lorrie Vogel
Former VP, Nike Material Science and Innovation

Abstract

Slow Down to Speed Up: Lead, Succeed, and Thrive in a 24/7 World is a powerful new resource for leaders from the C-Suite to the front line. Filled with innovative new approaches, pragmatic tools, and real-life success stories, this book tackles the universal challenge of getting better, faster, more sustainable results in a world of nonstop demands and constant connectivity.

Slow Down to Speed Up provides the concepts and tools to help leaders successfully strategize, prioritize, lead with purpose, find balance, and gain a competitive edge in today's fast-paced business environment. Based on Dr. Liz Bywater's 20 years of professional experience helping individuals, teams, and organizations thrive, the book contains real-world illustrations of the challenges faced by today's business leaders. Beyond that, it provides actionable guidance to help readers make the best decisions, create a proactive, future-focused work culture, catapult individual and team performance, and lead extraordinarily successful organizations.

Keywords

Business, Effectiveness, Leadership, Organizations, Performance, Pivot, Pivot Points, Proactive, Strategic, Strategic Pause, Success, Team, Thrive, Workplace

Contents

Acknowledgments..*xi*

Introduction...*xiii*

Part 1   **Slow Down**.. 1

Chapter 1   Racing to Results: What's Wrong with Going
Too Fast?..3

Chapter 2   Hitting the Brakes: Strategic Pauses and 36 Other
Ways to Slow Down...15

Chapter 3   Checking the Rearview Mirror: Pivot Points and
Reflections 25

Chapter 4   Setting Your Sights: What Do You Love, What Do
You Bring, and Where Are You Headed? 37

Part 2   **Speed Up!**.. 49

Chapter 5   Taking the Wheel: Do the Right Things, Make the
Best Decisions, Master Time 51

Chapter 6   Relax, Recharge, Refuel: You Can't Thrive If You Are
Running on Empty 67

Chapter 7   Hitting the Gas: Your Accelerating Success
Action Plan 73

Chapter 8   Tools for a Successful Pit Stop: Diagnostics,
Worksheets, and Bonus Items..77

Index *97*

Acknowledgments

Where do I begin thanking the many advisors, colleagues, clients, friends, and family members who generously supported me through the writing and publication of Slow Down to Speed Up? You have been truly indispensable. You've given me inspiration, direction, support, and a window into your most pressing leadership challenges. Without all of you, this book would have surely slowed down … but never sped up!

My heartfelt thanks go to:

Rob Zwettler and Business Expert Press, for quickly seeing the value in this work and guiding me through the publication process.

My wonderful clients, who've inspired me to create a roadmap for thriving in a 24/7 world, in which short-term results and rapid decisions can easily overshadow the long term. I've thoroughly enjoyed and grown from every aspect of our work.

The exceptional leaders who shared their personal stories, experiences, and advice with me (and you). Special thanks go to Danny DeAtley, Toby Massa, Bob Mauch, Rita McIntyre, Jeff Moody, Trish O'Keefe, Ryan Taggart, and Debbie Visconi.

My earliest reviewers, who gave of their time to take a sneak peek at the book and offer me feedback and insights: Dave Neu, Esperanza Neu, and Rob Wright.

Literary agents Esmond Harmsworth and Jane von Mehren, who guided me to fill these pages with a host of real-life success stories and practical tools for leadership success.

Mentors and colleagues who helped me recognize the importance of writing this book, offered me targeted advice, encouraged, and challenged me along the way: Alan Weiss, Lorraine Moore, Val Wright, Sarah Levitt, Phil Symchych, Noah Fleming, and countless other extraordinary colleagues in the Million Dollar Consulting community.

Editorial and process visuals assistants, Sarah Damberger and Caroline Niziol. I couldn't have gotten to the finish line without you!

Last but most assuredly not least, my remarkable friends and family. You inspire me to take a profound and personal stake in finding balance. Many thanks to my dear Dave, Anna and Jonathan; Mom and Dad; Leon, Lisa, and their incredible families; Robin and Glen; Steve and TeriLyn; and so many others. I feel incredibly fortunate to have you in my life.

Introduction

Without reflection, we go blindly on our way, creating more
unintended consequences,
and failing to achieve anything useful.

Margaret J. Wheatley

Slow Down to Speed Up is a new kind of resource for leaders from the C-Suite to the front line. This book will help you lead, succeed, and thrive amid the overwhelming pace of business and the nonstop demands on your time and energy. As you read this book and apply the principles, you will find yourself remarkably well equipped to increase personal, team, and organizational success.

I've written *Slow Down to Speed Up* for people just like you—leaders who are ready to stop putting out fires; leaders who refuse to continually react to the crisis du jour; leaders who are looking for a more thoughtful and strategic approach to the extraordinary work of leadership. This book will quickly become your go-to prompt to step out of the busyness of business and embrace a more considered and proactive stance. It will be your front-and-center handbook as you strategically target larger, more rewarding opportunities for yourself and your organization. You can use it as a roadmap, guiding you to the achievement of meaningful goals, heightened career satisfaction, and increased mastery over the complex and competing demands on your time.

To help you make the best decisions and get the right things done, I am giving you page upon page of targeted advice, plus an assortment of real-life success stories and practical techniques to help you slow down just long enough to develop a captivating vision and draw your path from today to tomorrow.

Slow Down to Speed Up is truly for leaders of all kinds—from Fortune 500 executives to non-profit directors, from private equity partners to serial entrepreneurs. Whether you're a community leader or a head of government, a seasoned mentor or an MBA student trying to master the "secret sauce" of leadership, you will benefit from these pragmatic principles and strategies.

Here's the bottom line. If you are a leader whose success requires getting results through smart, strategic decision-making, time mastery, and the ability to harness the collective contributions of a team, this book is for you.

Throughout the book, you will discover readily applied exercises along with real-life examples, a variety of challenges faced and successes achieved by some of my most successful clients: top-level executives in thriving organizations like Johnson & Johnson, Nike, Thomson Reuters, AmerisourceBergen, Bristol-Myers Squibb, and more. I have simply modified names and other identifying details to preserve the privacy of my clients.

I am delighted to share with you what I've observed and taught over the years, integrating more than a decade's work as a leadership expert and advisor to some of the world's most accomplished executives, and 20 years as a clinical psychologist, helping people live more successful, meaningful, and fulfilling lives. This book will show you how to master the tools of slowing down to reflect and plan before you take action. So you can stop reacting and start leading.

The book is written in two parts.

Part One, *Slow Down*, focuses on the challenge of getting results in a fast-paced world that demands quick decisions and rapid action. It provides the framework for taking your foot off the gas just long enough to thoughtfully set direction—building upon past experiences, personal strengths, and a clear vision of the future.

Part Two, *Speed Up*, teaches you how to move from reflection and planning into purposeful action. This is where the rubber meets the road. Here you will find an array of tools and techniques to clear through the clutter of daily decision-making, reduce overwhelm, and create the best possible outcomes.

After immersing yourself in Parts One and Two, you will have everything you need to take charge of your own success and lead your organization to extraordinary results. You will be equipped and ready to lead, succeed, and thrive in a 24/7 world!

PART ONE

Slow Down

CHAPTER 1

Racing to Results

What's Wrong with Going Too Fast?

In today's high velocity, always-on business environment, leaders like you are expected to make incredibly rapid decisions, work at a breakneck pace, and achieve exceptional results—all without losing a moment's time. Fast, faster, and faster yet. That's the mandate from customers, colleagues, managers, business partners, boards, investors, and any number of other important stakeholders. Yet no individual, team, or organization can consistently and sustainably do its best when working at a frenetic pace or under constant, intense pressure.

Decisiveness is an essential leadership trait. Hasty decision-making? Not so much. Getting results quickly is important. Yet the pursuit of short-term wins can undermine a focus on longer-term growth. And an excessive attention to the daily tasks can get in the way of creating long-term strategic impact.

My client, Randy, who leads a team of scientific writers and researchers, put it this way:

> As a leader, my responsibility is basically to look at the business in two to three year increments. I know already where we are this year. It's more about looking at the next three. But because the teams are focused so much on the day-to-day, I sometimes have the feeling I can't look ahead, even speaking in months—one month, two months, three months out—because we can't get out of our own way day to day. I frequently hear, "I have to get this done, I have to get it out the door." And that's all true, but let's at least look at the next quarter. What will be complete by then, and what can we build on?

You don't want to minimize what is happening day to day. The daily work has to get done and our teams are very focused on that. But my job is to look at the business and say, "Here's where we are with our initiatives. Let's take a look now a couple of months down the line. What can be developed and what shall we be thinking about now, so that we can talk to our clients about the additional challenges and opportunities on their horizon?"

That's the focus of the work we did when you came in to help us. And it created a definite mindset shift. Rather than just focusing so much on the day or week ahead, we're moving now to months and that's been incredibly helpful to us. It's not just about survival of the day, but much more about the vision for a particular client, and making sure we never take our eye off it.

There's no doubt, it is important to be responsive to clients. And certainly, you need to get the immediate work done. Even beyond that, it's good to be agile in today's business climate, and that can require moving pretty fast. Just remember, if you move too quickly, too often—if you chronically rush to results, react rather than anticipate, focus on short-term activities but neglect the long-term view—you will miss important opportunities for growth.

You are also going to make mistakes—many of them repetitive, most of them avoidable. Sometimes these will be modest-enough mistakes. Ideally, you will learn from them and move on. But if you are in the habit of continually going too fast, you will make the kind of major mistakes that put you, your company, customers, and investors at risk. These mistakes may require millions of dollars to remedy. They may also cost you valued clients, talent, revenue, and reputation.

There is a solution, rest assured, and it's right at your fingertips. It's a matter of shifting your balance. Adjust your focus from near-term actions to the longer-term, strategic view. Be more proactive than reactive. Slow down to learn from past successes and failures. Refuse to become embroiled in daily fire-fighting. Shift the balance and you will find it so much easier to advance while preventing mistakes large and small.

What's Wrong with Moving Too Fast?

When leaders move too quickly, they often pay a steep price.

My client, Dianne, knows this all too well. Not long ago, Dianne nearly undermined an opportunity to win the largest and most rewarding piece of work she'd proposed in 30 years. Although a recognized expert in her field, with a vast portfolio of successful projects, Dianne was at a critical moment when she came to ask for my help. She needed my strategic guidance to help her salvage this landmark project. Winning this work would have immediate rewards and also create a model for new work with clients across the country.

Dianne's project was in jeopardy because she was moving too fast. Amid an extremely busy schedule and facing a rapidly approaching deadline, Dianne had made some serious mistakes: She'd invited the wrong partner to collaborate on her project, and then inadvertently handed him the reins. She'd arranged a call with her buyer to discuss objectives and options rather than scheduling time with him, in person, to address his questions and concerns. She'd accepted unrealistic client deadlines on an array of projects and now was under pressure to get too much done in too little time. She felt overwhelmed and out of control. And it was beginning to take a toll. Her oversights and missteps nearly caused her to lose control of this project. She sought my help in a state of alarm, sensing that she was about to blow up the biggest deal of her life.

As Dianne and I began our work, it quickly became apparent to me just how much she had in common with the Fortune 500 executives I advise every day. Like them, and perhaps like you, she consistently had more to do than time in which to do it. She had a penchant for taking on too much. She rarely set limits and she almost never said no. She was overworked, over-scheduled, and often overwhelmed.

Dianne had long attempted to wrestle the intense demands of a growing business by running just a little faster, sleeping just a little less, juggling just a bit more, and always at her own expense. She rarely felt fully in charge of her time or her business. And yet, all the while, she had a palpable desire to be more effective as she grew her company, helped her customers in new and transformational ways, and pursued her legacy of leaving a deep and lasting impact on the world.

This was a real dilemma. If she kept going as she had been, incredibly busy, overcommitted, often stretched to the limits, her business would stagnate and ultimately decline. She would remain mired in mid-level projects that paid far too little for the value she brought. Her clients would lose faith in her and her formerly stellar reputation would spiral downward. In fact, some clients had begun to express concern about Dianne's lateness to appointments and inconsistency in meeting deadlines. If things didn't improve quickly, Dianne's project would slip through her fingers. Her vision would remain elusive, her legacy unfulfilled.

In my work with Dianne and hundreds of other leaders, I've seen the same dynamic time and time again. In a well-intended effort to get rapid results in a fast-paced world, leaders rush to decisions, say yes too often, and favor the short-term. They move too quickly and make preventable mistakes. Results suffer, stress mounts, and success remains out of reach.

So Many Decisions . . .

Today's leaders make an astonishing number of decisions every day—decisions that require time for thoughtful reflection. Yet, if you are like many business leaders, you find yourself making important decisions on the fly, often without enough time for thorough consideration or requisite input from others. It's an unfortunate dynamic, and it can lead directly to failure.

My client, Tina, a seasoned executive at a multinational health care company, has seen this firsthand. She's lived through a multiple examples of the mistakes that resulted from rushed decisions and inadequate stakeholder.

Several years ago, Tina was asked to salvage a major initiative on the verge of collapse. It was an important project, involving the development of a new IT system to help the company process critical safety data for the FDA. By the time Tina was brought in to help, this key initiative was already a year behind schedule.

The problem was this: To be properly implemented, developers of the new system required input from stakeholders across multiple functions. It was an essential step in getting the system to function properly. But in an effort to hit an overly aggressive deadline, the project had been hurried along. And while things moved along well enough at first, significant problems arose over time. With the lack of communication and coordination, mistakes were made and relationships became strained. Major problems were overlooked. Eventually, the entire system had to be rebuilt from the bottom up. It required an additional year and $2 million to finally arrive at a solution that worked. Time had been wasted, money squandered, and collaborations strained. Yet it had all been quite preventable. A little upfront time for key conversations would have made all the difference.

. . . So Little Time

It has been estimated that, on average, each of us makes 3,500 decisions a day. Every one of these decisions, large and small, takes up mental energy, leading to cognitive fatigue and impacting effectiveness. The more decisions we make, the more depleted we become, and the less adept at making outstanding choices.

Even something that seems straightforward—responding to e-mail—requires an array of decisions, such as:

- *Should I reply by e-mail, or pick up the phone, or walk down the hall for a face-to-face conversation?*
- *Should I send my reply now or later?*
- *How many people should be copied?*
- *How much background must I provide?*
- *Do I add a warm greeting to soften the tone?*
- *Should I include a comprehensive view or just provide the highlights ?*

Of course, we don't consciously think through the nuances of every decision. But the fact is, we are making decision upon decision, whether consciously or not, all day long. This abundance of daily decisions requires our attention, energy, and valuable time.

As you probably know firsthand, e-mail alone can eat up hours of precious time. The average manager receives more than 120 e-mails each day, and senior executives often face a barrage of 500+ daily e-mail messages. All that time and energy spent fielding a constant barrage of e-mail translates to decreased time and energy for more important decisions and actions throughout the day.

The Very Real Problem of E-mail

In early 2016, I started working with Mark, a new Vice President of Research and Development for a rapidly growing medical device company. Still just a few months in the role and new to the company, Mark felt energized and excited but also overwhelmed. He was navigating a new job and trying to learn the ropes of a complex business. He'd inherited a disorganized team that required a great deal of his time and attention. He had a demanding boss with whom he had to align on goals, priorities, and expectations. He had literally dozens of important stakeholders with whom he had to rapidly establish credibility, trust, and communication—the foundations of a strong working relationship.

Mark also had several key projects to advance. And in the midst of it all, hundreds of e-mails cluttered his inbox each day. To deal with it, he would begin his workday before sunrise and dedicate the first 2 hours of the day to clearing his inbox. He'd send replies where needed and scroll through a virtual sea of "FYI" messages. Needless to say, this took a great deal of time and often pulled him away from more important matters.

Mark believed his early morning e-mail routine was a necessary sacrifice, the only way to create time and space for the rest of his daily activities. But it simply wasn't sustainable. He was getting by on less than 5 hours of sleep each night, fueling up on a diet of coffee and junk food, growing impatient with his team and increasingly stressed by daily challenges.

To help him gain control, I taught Mark a straightforward approach to mastering e-mail overwhelms. As a result, he was able to enjoy an extra hour of sleep each night. With more rest, he began to arrive at work with greater energy, focus, and patience. He made better decisions, built stronger relationships, and led his team to top results. (See Chapter 5 for my *Targeted E-mail Reduction System*.)

Hasty Decisions

Rushing to a decision can lead to a feeling of regret, even when the outcome is positive. When we fail to fully consider the pros, cons, and implications of a decision, we tend to feel dissatisfied with the choice we've made. That dissatisfaction can engender stress, which may seriously impair the ability to make good decisions.

Does this sound familiar? As a busy executive, you regularly have too much to do and too little time in which to do it. You need help and you need it fast. Perhaps there is pressure to quickly bring on a new employee. As a result, you rush the process. In your haste, you fail to slow down to thoroughly assess whether the candidate is really the best fit: for the job, your team, company, and culture. That kind of fast-paced hiring frequently leads to trouble.

Hastily hired employees tend to flounder and fail, often exiting just as quickly as they'd been brought in. Such new hires may not have enough time to learn the ropes. In many cases, they quit or get fired before they've had the chance to understand the business, get to know the team, figure out how to navigate the culture, or get the results for which they were hired.

These rapid hires can cost a great deal. Losing an executive costs a company, on average, 1.5–2x that employee's annual salary. It costs even by way of lost opportunities, disrupted collaborations, fractured relationships, wasted training, decreased team cohesiveness, damaged reputation and reduced morale.

This is something my client, John, knows all too well. When I first met John, he had far too much on his plate to be fully effective. Working at a large tech company, John had a number of important projects underway. And while he was sufficiently energetic, bright, and visionary to manage all of these initiatives, he was seriously understaffed. He needed to hire additional employees and he needed them fast.

So John did what many managers do. He screened a handful of resumes, met with some promising candidates, spent about an hour with each one, then came to a rapid decision based on his gut feeling. He proceeded to offer his most important role to the most appealing candidate.

The problem is this. Working amid intense busyness, pressure, and frequent fire-fighting, John hadn't allotted adequate time to get to know the job candidates well. And while most people can do well enough in a 1-hour job interview, it takes longer than 60 minutes to learn what lies beneath a first impression.

Beyond rushing the interview itself, John hadn't slowed down to thoroughly consider the personality style most important for success in the role. Was he looking for someone bold and assertive, or thoughtful and reflective? Inclusive and communicative, or a heads-down individual contributor? Did he need someone who would lead from the front, cheer from the sidelines, or quietly follow directions? He hadn't given it sufficient thought and, as a result, he didn't have a keen eye out for best-fit attributes among his interviewees.

John thought he was doing the right thing by making a quick decision and acting without delay. He made his choice in good faith and trusted it would work out well.

Unfortunately, it didn't. John's new hire, Steven, lacked the executive presence and emotional intelligence required to build strong relationships and establish credibility with the management team. Although Steven didn't see it himself, he was failing to win the hearts and minds of the stakeholders most important to his success. Lacking strong relationships and support, he began to sink.

While John remained focused on other priorities, Steven was descending into failure. Distracted by conflicting demands on his time, John had left Steven to his own devices, neglecting to give him clear guidance or help him navigate the complex dynamics of the executive team. Before long, it was too late. The executive team told John that Steven had been a poor choice and was now an impediment to progress. John's judgment was called into question. His credibility took a hit. He decided to let Steven go mere months after bringing him in.

As we worked together, I helped John recognize the importance of slowing down: taking the time to think beyond the resumes and thoughtfully reflect on the intangible factors most important for success. As a result, he's now making astute hiring decisions, demonstrating his ability to select the right people and set them up for success. He can now delegate more of the implementation of his initiatives, knowing the work will be handled effectively by his growing team. His time and energy have been freed up, giving him time to focus on vision, strategy, and influence. These changes have allowed him to contribute to key decisions at the most senior levels of the company.

Regrettable Repetitions

When leaders act too quickly, they are bound to make mistakes. Repeated mistakes. Costly mistakes. Preventable mistakes. They're what I call *regrettable repetitions.*

Take Jennifer, a division president for a midsize manufacturer. When she and I first met, her objective was to achieve 20 percent growth in 18 months. It was an ambitious but achievable goal, if only she could steer her organization out of its own way.

The greatest obstacle to double digit growth wasn't the competitive landscape. It wasn't the rigorous regulatory environment, the challenges of customer acquisition, or the ability to attract top talent. The real barrier to growth was the mistakes that Jennifer's organization kept making; the same sort of mistakes, over and over again. Within the past year alone, repeated errors or regrettable repetitions had cost the company millions of dollars and dramatically hindered growth. Jennifer was extremely frustrated. She knew something had to change.

I've seen it time and time again. Executives, teams, and organizations that move too quickly often pay a price. But those who learn to slow down to develop a more thoughtful path forward usually succeed. When leaders learn to pause and reflect before acting, they make better decisions, achieve faster results, and avert the kind of mistakes that take precious time, energy, and political capital to correct. Slowing the pace, paradoxically enough, is the most direct and fruitful path to stellar outcomes, exemplary leadership, personal accomplishment, and a thriving organization.

For Jennifer, the solution required slowing her team down to do three things:

1. Consider the approach.
   - *What are we trying to achieve?*
   - *What's the most direct and effective path there?*

   By taking the time to be strategic, thoughtful, and proactive, your team will dramatically accelerate results and minimize preventable errors.

2. Anticipate obstacles.
   - *What can get in the way of steady progress?*
   - *What have our past experiences taught us, and how can we apply that knowledge today?*
   - *Which mistakes have been made and how can they be avoided in the future?*
   - *How can we solve for the potential difficulties that lie ahead?*

3. Share success stories. The best teams discuss wins with one another on a regular basis (such as in team meetings) and ad-hoc. This allows them to apply and adapt successful approaches to new opportunities. As a bonus, it provides a venue for recognizing and celebrating accomplishments. It doesn't take much time and the return is extraordinary.

I helped Jennifer launch a new approach, to increase effectiveness and decrease errors, by conducting a 2-day *strategic pause* with her leadership team. Together, we helped the team slow down to reflect on goals, priorities, opportunities, and challenges. We took the time to identify accelerators and obstacles. The team worked creatively and collaboratively, developing ways to learn from past successes and prevent regrettable repetitions. We developed a high-impact plan of action with clear accountabilities, timelines, and pathways of communication. The team committed to taking a more strategic and proactive approach as they paved an accelerated path to growth.

Jennifer and the team walked away from their strategic pause with a renewed sense of confidence, purpose, and optimism. Relationships were strengthened, communication improved and trust skyrocketed. In the coming months, errors decreased dramatically. The team strategic pause got the attention of other business leaders who quickly sought to replicate the approach.

What Happens When Leaders Slow Down

Dennis, a talented IT executive, came to understand the importance and impact of slowing down. When he and I began working together, he had a reputation as a leader with exceptional skills and a strategic mindset. He had years of valuable experience behind him and was at the helm of a large department.

In the course of his 18 years at the company, Dennis had received a series of promotions. As he rose through the ranks, his technical abilities became less relevant to success than his ability to build relationships and influence an array of stakeholders. But with so much on his plate, Dennis struggled to let go. He frequently dove into the technical aspects of the work, while neglecting his most important relationships. Somewhat uncomfortable in social situations, Dennis would avoid company events where he could network with other top leaders. He preferred to keep his head down and get the work done.

He readily acknowledged that the technical work came more naturally and comfortably than spending time with colleagues and business partners. But leading in a matrixed, relationship-driven company meant he'd have to look up from the daily tasks and get in front of commercial peers who could support his initiatives and advance his agenda.

When Dennis adopted my *Stakeholder Priority Plan* (SPP), he found that he could more readily identify and prioritize time with his most important stakeholders. He created a targeted approach to rapidly improve relationships, with a laser focus on the people who held the greatest potential impact on his success. (See Chapter 5 to learn how to implement my *Stakeholder Priority Plan*.) His improved approach helped him become a more influential leader. He was able to garner support and funding for his initiatives, elevate his leadership stature, and attract an array of new opportunities, each of which entailed a promotion. He earned a performance rating in the top 5 percent in his company, along with a significant raise and bonus to reward his accomplishments.

CHAPTER 2

Hitting the Brakes

Strategic Pauses and 36 Other Ways to Slow Down

There's no doubt about it. Quick results and rapid decisions are essential in today's fast-paced, 24/7 world. And if you slow down for too long, you may well be left in the dust. But if you chronically go too fast . . . you will win the sprint and lose the marathon.

How can a thoughtful leader resist the pull of intense pressure to hurry up and get things done? Paradoxically, it starts with taking a pause—a *strategic pause.*

A strategic pause is a deliberate step back from the swirling torrent of daily activity to take a calmer, more thoughtful approach. It's a way to protect time so you can consider how to tackle a challenge, advance your goals, make stellar decisions, create new opportunities, and drive to exceptional outcomes.

My most successful clients have learned to periodically take their foot off the accelerator, to reflect on their most meaningful opportunities and challenges, top strengths and vulnerabilities, strategy and vision, pressing priorities, and most compelling goals. They've come to see that stepping back is the key to success: for themselves, their teams, and their companies.

I don't have to convince you that in our fast-paced world, taking a pause can feel implausible, impractical, or self-indulgent. I get it. Believe me, I understand how busy you are, and I know how much pressure you're under. Like you, I sometimes find myself faced with back-to-back meetings, nonstop e-mails and voice messages, and the kind of excessive busyness that leads to a sense of overwhelm and exhaustion by the end of the day. I know how that feels, and I recognize how hard it can be to slow down.

But the truth is, neither you nor I can effectively go on this way, day after day. There's just too steep a price for continually operating at such an intense pace. Beyond the fatigue and stress that accompany rushed days, our decision-making process begins to break down. Rather than consistently making well-considered choices, we start to make some pretty important decisions without conscious deliberation. In the face of too much to do and too little time to think, we begin running on autopilot.

Think about the last time you got in your car and distractedly took a wrong turn or wound up in the wrong place. How could this have happened? After all, you've probably taken the same path dozens, maybe even hundreds of times. And you generally get where you've intended to go, without pausing to make the multitude of in-the-moment decisions. In fact, unless you are a new driver, you rarely consciously ponder your next move. You don't need to think about where to turn and you don't stop to reflect on the many micro-decisions that lead to important actions: slamming the brakes to avoid traffic ahead, looking over your shoulder for cars in your blind spot before changing lanes, hitting the gas to merge into the flow of traffic. You do these things without pausing or taking conscious note of your decisions—and it almost always works out.

Except sometimes it doesn't. Sometimes you find yourself taking a wrong turn, inadvertently getting on the highway heading south instead of north. You could be halfway to your office before you remember the meeting being held across town. Or, even worse, you've become so automatic in your actions that you fail to notice the brake lights up ahead—and you suddenly find yourself careening into an unforeseen traffic jam.

That's the problem with moving forward without thinking. Although we often do well enough, as we rush through our days and lead our organizations, at other times, we don't do very well at all. And unless we take the time to slow down—to thoughtfully consider what we are trying to achieve and how we are going to achieve it—we may just find ourselves stuck, lost, or landing at an unintended destination.

As a leader, you have an opportunity, and the responsibility, to take control of the wheel. After all, it's your job to effectively navigate the path to success—for yourself, your team, and your company. And that requires taking a pause—a strategic pause.

Remember, a strategic pause is a deliberate break in your day (or week, month, quarter, or year). It is a reflection break, a time to stop doing and start thinking. It's your time to slow down, calm down, and create space for uninterrupted strategic contemplation.

You can also make use of a strategic pause to clear your head, build your confidence, steady yourself for an uncomfortable conversation or hone your messaging before an important presentation. You will find it's far more effective take a pause—to sit quietly, think, review some notes and take a few deep breaths—than it is to fly from meeting to meeting without a break.

Strategic pauses are important but they may not come naturally, especially if you are under pressure to meet deadlines, hit the numbers, and get results fast. As a result, these pauses won't happen unless you make them a priority, building them into your schedule and protecting them from a multitude of competing demands.

Take my word for it; it's worth the effort. In fact, strategic pauses are so essential to effective leadership, you should make them part of your daily routine. Now before you close the book in protest—because you can't fathom finding time each day to slow down and think—be assured, this isn't something that has to take a whole lot of time. In fact, a modest 15-minute pause can do wonders. Pick a time that works for you. Maybe your best time is when you wake up in the morning, before you get out of bed and grab your first cup of coffee. Or perhaps it's better to arrive at the office 15 minutes early to ensure time to pause without impacting the rest of the day's commitments.

If mornings don't work well, set aside time midday or just before leaving the office. You get the idea. Find a time that works—and stick to it. Even on your busiest days, you can (and must) find pockets of time to pause and think.

Your strategic pauses can be used in a variety of ways. You can use them to thoughtfully reflect on your priorities for the day or week ahead. You can use them to prompt yourself to be more present, engaged, or vocal in your next meeting. You can use them to think through the feedback you're about to provide to a team member, zeroing in on the best wording and tone for a productive conversation. Or you can take a strategic pause to gain some emotional distance, as you contend with the stress that can readily arise from daily challenges or conflicts.

As you pause, keep a pen and pad by your side to capture thoughts, concerns, and potential solutions. If an intrusive thought finds its way into your mind—a pending presentation, an important meeting, a simmering conflict with a colleague, problems at home—simply write it down and bring yourself back into the present moment. This will help you push aside distractions and focus on the immediate topic of reflection.

Here are a few prompts to help you make the most of your strategic pauses. See Chapter 8 for a worksheet to help you capture your thoughts.

- *What are my top priorities for the day? the week? the month, quarter, or year?*
- *What must I absolutely accomplish today? What's my plan to get it done?*
- *Which activities can I delegate, delay, or dismiss altogether? (Before agreeing to any request, ask yourself: Me, not me? Now, later, never? See Chapter 6 for more.)*
- *How will I resolve an unpleasant conflict with my boss, peer, or customer?*
- *What was today's greatest success?*
- *How can I build on that success—tomorrow, next week, in the coming month, quarter, or year?*
- *What could I have done differently and how will I apply what I've learned today for greater impact in the future?*

If you need some time to calm or center yourself:

- *Shut your office door. Give your assistant explicit instructions: No non-emergency interruptions for the next 15 minutes.*
- *Turn off all electronic notifications—no pings, vibrations, or ringtones to distract you.*
- *Listen to something that relaxes you.*
- *Stand and stretch. Relax your shoulders. Unclench your jaw.*
- *Breathe. Try a 4-second inhale, 7-second hold, 8-second exhale.*
- *Allow yourself a few minutes to relax and regroup.*

These ideas are just the tip of the iceberg. Use the specific prompts and techniques you like and create some of your own. Remember, strategic pauses are not wasted time. They are neither an indulgence nor fluff. On the contrary, they will help you to do your best work, as you create space for thoughtful decision-making. Build them into your calendar and advise your team to do the same. Prioritize and protect the time. It's really that important.

When I introduced the concept of the strategic pause to my client, Pat, she told me that she was far too busy to even try. Although she conceptually recognized the value of taking a strategic and proactive approach to her work, she couldn't see herself carving out time to pause. Over the course of our work, however, she began to cautiously experiment, pausing on occasion before committing to a daily routine.

In anticipation of an upcoming meeting with her CEO, for example, she knew it was essential to sharpen her message and present with poise and confidence. So she began to set aside small blocks of time in the weeks preceding that important meeting. She refused to allow distractions to pull her away and, in these uninterrupted moments, developed a clear approach. She took the time to craft and practice her message, reviewing and revising, relying on me as a thought partner and mock CEO with whom she could practice. She worked out the initial kinks in the presentation and developed newfound self-confidence.

When the time came to meet with the CEO, Pat hit it out of the park. He was impressed with the presentation and with Pat's confident manner. Her manager was delighted, too. Having experienced this kind of success, Pat now builds strategic pauses into each day, prioritizing these breaks as an invaluable tool in her leadership toolkit.

Like Pat, once you've had a bit of practice and evidence of the value of pausing, your strategic pauses will become second nature. Whether you use them daily, weekly, quarterly, or ad-hoc, you will find that these pauses become natural, automatic, and downright indispensable.

Let me tell you about another client of mine, a bright, ambitious sales leader named Ian. He and I began working together days after he'd been passed over for a coveted promotion.

Following 8 years at the helm of a thriving mid-sized business, Ian had taken an active role in the sale and integration of that organization into a Fortune 500 company. He'd never worked in such a large, complex organization, but he was a confident leader who knew his value. He was eager to introduce exciting ideas and drive innovation at the parent company. When the opportunity arose to lead a large business unit and play a key role on the management team, he immediately raised his hand.

No one at the parent company doubted whether Ian could lead. They knew he had run a successful business, inspired his organization, and produced terrific results. They'd seen the loyalty of his employees, who freely conveyed their admiration, trust, and dedicated followership.

At issue was Ian's ability to present himself as a "buttoned up" corporate executive, a leader with the finesse to influence at the highest levels of this large, conservative, and politically complex company. It was not a matter of smarts or substance but of style and fit.

Ian was a bold and incredibly confident communicator who sometimes came across as overly self-assured. He was passionate. He was spontaneous. He was genuine. At times, he was irreverent. These qualities had served him well in winning the hearts of his employees. They loved his openness, authenticity, and spontaneity. However, the management team had concerns about his off-the-cuff, say-what's-on-your-mind, sometimes unorthodox approach. They weren't confident that he had the executive presence of a Fortune 500 leader. And so, they gave the job to another candidate.

To be more effective, Ian had to learn to pause before he spoke. He had to thoughtfully consider whether, when, and how to express himself with top executives at his new company. This called for a major increase in self-reflection and self-monitoring. It required a willingness to be vulnerable enough to ask others for real-time feedback. It took practice and it took time.

During the course of our work, Ian learned to slow down. Instead of charging full speed ahead, he took time to pause and self-reflect. He learned to dial his intensity up and bring it down as needed. Before long, he became more effective across a variety of situations, with different audiences and in an array of venues. Ultimately, this more thoughtful approach became second nature. Ian increased his executive presence and rapidly elevated his credibility. Within a year, he had another chance at promotion. This time, he landed it. He's been thriving in his new role ever since.

Striking the Balance

Slowing down doesn't mean you should stagnate. The fact is, if you've slowed down too much, for too long, you may just be stuck in the mud. And that's as much of a problem as moving too quickly. Slowing down to speed up is about taking just enough time to thoughtfully reflect, strategize, and plan—as you set yourself up for accelerated impact, increased influence, and lasting success.

The challenge is this. If you are drowning in pressure to get immediate results—let's say, you have to get an important report to a client by 5 p.m. or you need to reach an aggressive sales target by the end of the month— you may be strongly inclined to focus on short-term achievements at the expense of longer-term success. There's a balance to strike. This holds true for individual leaders, teams, and entire companies. Here's what Bob Mauch, Group President, Pharmaceutical Distribution and Strategic Global Sourcing, AmerisourceBergen Corporation, had to say about balancing short-term objectives and long-term goals:

> In every month and quarter there are initiatives to be success-fully completed. You earn the right to drive on those short-term activities by clearly communicating a very healthy foundation for the long term. Of course, we have to make our numbers. We're a big, publicly traded company. Not making your numbers is not an option. But we're not just chasing the quarter. That's just one step along the way to achieving our longer term goals.

If you or your team have a project that requires rapid response—a client who needs your immediate help, a regulatory agency demanding rapid response, or a sales target that cannot be missed—then your atten-tion must go to those pressing priorities first. On the other hand, if you attend to the here-and-now but neglect the longer view or bigger picture, you will do well enough for a while. But will you, or your organization, thrive over the course of time? Not likely.

During a recent visit to the salon (because sometimes you have to slow down to look your best!), I had a conversation with a seasoned stylist named Lauren. She was interested in the book and related immediately to the concept of slowing down to speed up. As we talked, she shared with me her personal challenge of balancing short-term objectives (making more money for immediate needs) with long-term success (retaining clients and gaining referrals).

Lauren earns her living on a commission basis. The more clients she sees, the more money she makes. When financial pressures hit, like when she needs to replace her hot water heater or save for next month's vacation, she is more likely to squeeze in a few extra clients. At these times, she will accept walk-in appointments and skip lunch to see as many people as she can. This allows her to rapidly increase revenue in the short-term but it comes at a price. On her busiest days, she finds herself depleted and hungry, having reserved no time to rest or refuel. Moreover, on over-scheduled days, she can't give her long-time clients the extra attention to which they've grown accustomed. Ultimately, this translates to unhappy customers, fewer repeat visits and referrals, and less money in her pocket. It's a short-term gain with a long-term cost.

36 Actions to Accelerate Success

If you're still not convinced that slowing down is a good use of time, check out the ideas below. I've given you 36 actions, and that's just to get you started. These pauses in your typical daily routine will help you achieve better, faster results. All it takes is a modest investment of upfront time and effort. I'll give you the first five here. Turn to Chapter 8 for the full list of 36 Actions to Accelerate.

Aessess:

1. *Your current situation, challenge, or opportunity.* Examine it from a variety of angles. Is this a near-term priority? Will it help you advance your strategic objectives? When and how will you approach it for the greatest impact and advantage?

2. *The competition.* In which ways do the competition have an advantage? What are your competitor's gaps or weaknesses? How can you differentiate and elevate yourself to gain advantage and increase market share?

3. *Your team.* Look closely at talent, individual and collective performance, potential, behavior, collaboration, communication, conflict resolution, and trust. Do you have the right people in the right roles doing the right things? Is your team performing at the highest possible level? Do you need to make any changes to structure or staffing to accelerate impact and improve outcomes?

4. *Your personal brand, reputation, and credibility within the organization.* Have you earned the respect and recognition of colleagues, managers, and partners? Do others see you as you see yourself? How will you build upon the good and address shortcomings?

5. *Your reputation with customers and clients.* How are you perceived? Are the relationships as strong as they need to be? Are there concerns or problems to be addressed? How can you leverage, change, or improve your reputation?

CHAPTER 3

Checking the Rearview Mirror

Pivot Points and Reflections

As you begin to take strategic pauses, you will increase your effectiveness, reduce stress, improve decision-making, and prevent the repetition of costly errors. Yet, if you're like many of my clients—bright, accomplished executives with demanding jobs and jam-packed days—you may find yourself in a role or on a path that emerged by happenstance rather than design. You may be doing work that you like but don't love. Perhaps you are tapping into some of your strengths but neglecting what you truly bring to the table.

Perhaps you haven't allowed yourself the time to thoughtfully consider where you started and where you've been. Maybe you haven't slowed down to reflect upon the people, decisions, and events exerting the greatest impact on where you are today. Maybe you are aren't crystal clear about where you want to go next: Which role or opportunity should you pursue? Where do you want to be in a year, 5 years, or as you approach retirement?

That sort of self-reflection may seem an indulgence, particularly if you are under intense pressure to get things done. Time is limited and you are genuinely busy. In today's 24/7 world, it can be hard to keep up.

Trust me; this is worth the time. As you get know yourself better, by reviewing your past, crystallizing what you bring to the table, and sorting out what's been holding your back, you will become a better leader and more successful business person. You will build upon strengths, pursue your most gratifying work, and leap over the hurdles in your way.

I've developed an exercise to help you rapidly increase insight and self-knowledge. It requires little more than an investment of your time and the willingness to look in the rearview mirror. I call this exercise *Pivot Points.*

Start by selecting a point of entry. Depending upon how far back you want to go, you can start in childhood, college, early career, or later. Look at the events, experiences, and key decisions that have shaped who you are and how you lead. Take out a pad and pen and start with some simple notes about your past. Don't censor, just write whatever comes to mind. Some considerations are:

- *Childhood/family*
- *Culture/religion*
- *Relationships with friends/teachers/mentors*
- *Education*
- *Jobs, career decisions, achievements*
- *Marriage/family*
- *Health/fitness*
- *Community*
- *Professional/personal development*

* To use Pivot Points to reflect on a specific business challenge, consider the following:

- *The history of the challenge: Where did it start and how did the situation evolve?*
- *Team dynamics: What's helping or hindering progress, mitigating or perpetuating the problem?*
- *Strategic priorities: Where does this challenge or opportunity fit into your strategy?*
- *Milestones/achievements: Are these the correct milestones? Are the timelines sound?*
- *Resources: What do you have, what do you need, how can you get more?*
- *Obstacles/solutions*

Now ask yourself:

- *What has been the impact of each pivotal event and decision along the way?*
- *Which of these Pivot Points have been transformational? Which have had a meaningful or profound impact on who I am and how I lead?*
- *How have I responded to my unique set of experiences, opportunities, successes, and failures?*
- *Am I actively learning from experience—or simply repeating familiar yet ineffective patterns?*
- *Am I (or my team or company) repeating the same mistakes time and again?*
- *Which Pivot Points reflect a success or an achievement? Which ones have been a source of disappointment or regret?*

Here is a blank template to use when reflecting upon your path. For now, don't worry about sorting your Pivotal Successes from your Pivotal Regrets. We'll get to that next. For now, simply use the above prompts to guide your reflections.

Pivot Point	Impact

Pivotal Successes

As I work with my clients to identify their Pivot Points, we see that they generally fall into one of two buckets—*Pivotal Successes* and *Pivotal Regrets*. Because I am a firm believer that we grow most quickly and efficiently by building on strengths and replicating success, that's where we focus much of our attention. We look closely at Pivotal Successes.

Pivotal Successes are those events or decisions that have had a positive impact on your success, happiness, or both. Examples include: academic and professional recognition and awards, promotions, leadership positions, international assignments, or even resigning from a dead-end job. Other Pivotal Successes include running a marathon, marrying a supportive spouse, joining a non-profit board—you get the idea.

Think about your life and history. Identify each of the positive experiences, influences, and decisions—the Pivotal Successes—that you might otherwise ignore or take for granted. Consider, for example, the impact of your early relationships—with parents, siblings, teachers, grandparents, neighbors, cousins, and childhood friends. Reflect on your years as a student, front line employee, new executive or budding entrepreneur, spouse, parent, friend or community leader. Who and what were the positive influences? And where did you truly shine?

Here's an example. Trish O'Keefe was recently promoted to the role of president of Morristown Memorial Hospital. The promotion has been a crowning moment in her career, a culmination of the many experiences, decisions, and pivots she's made throughout her 30-year career and stemming from poignant childhood influences, relationships, and opportunities. Trish told me about some of the early influences that played a role in becoming a top-tier executive:

> I never envisioned myself to be president, but I had wonderful role models. When I was going to school, most females were either going for nursing, social work, or education. I had three nurses in my family, including my mom, who was clearly my mentor. When she went back to school, she was one of only two women in the Nursing Home Administration track. As a child, I would

go with her to the nursing home where she eventually became Nursing Home Administrator.

Like my mom, I always wanted to do something with people, with patients. I started working in that nursing home, first volunteering and then as a nurse's aid, learning a lot from the people there. I loved to sit and listen to the men who had been in World War II, hearing their stories and learning a great deal. I had an interest in those stories from a leadership perspective. But did I ever think I'd become a president of the hospital? No, because there were not many female presidents, let alone a nurse president existing at that time. I credit my mother for serving as a role model in my young years.

Check out the following list of Pivotal Successes. Which of these rings true? And which other experiences, influences, decisions, or pivots can you add?

- *Raised in a supportive family*
- *Had a role model or mentor*
- *Traveled to interesting places*
- *Had a strong connection to religious or civic community*
- *Went to top-tier university or graduate school*
- *Married a supportive spouse*

Beyond the life events that have influenced you, look at the successes you've had in dealing with leadership opportunities and challenges. These might include:

- *Took an international assignment, learned to leverage global opportunities and address cross-cultural challenges*
- *Led a key initiative*
- *Developed/implemented a breakthrough strategy*
- *Led my team or organization to stellar outcomes*
- *Achieved top market share or industry status*

Pivotal Successes	Impact
_____	_____
_____	_____
_____	_____
_____	_____
_____	_____

Begin to fill in your Pivotal Successes below. Don't be needlessly humble. Give yourself credit where credit is due. Pay close attention to the relationships, events, and decisions that helped you get to where you are today. Remember, this is the good stuff. These positive influences can be a powerful catapult to exceptional leadership and personal achievement.

To give you an example of how this works, here are a few of my own Pivotal Successes.

My Pivot Points: Pivotal Successes

Pivot point	Impact
Parents emphasized education	Instilled a lifelong love of learning
Took youth leadership roles	Established my love of leadership
Attended excellent college/ graduate school	Got a stellar education, met diverse people, broadened my POV
Earned my PhD in Clinical Psychology	Contributed deeply to my understanding of people, relationships, behavior, communication, teams, and leadership
Had/have outstanding mentors	Helped me apply my expertise in people to help executives improve leadership and drive commercial success
Started working with Fortune 100 execs	Helped me make a pivotal career transition: From clinician/ psychotherapist to leadership expert; allowed me to form strong professional relationships with CEOs and other business leaders
Joined a global community of experts	Gave me the opportunity to advance thought leadership with the world's top consultants even as I continually learn and grow
Supportive spouse and children	Lots of encouragement from the family and all the motivation I could ever need to keep helping others and growing my business

I haven't listed every Pivotal Success here, but I think you can see where I'm going. Take your time with this activity and be sure to celebrate your achievements as you reflect on the most rewarding, exciting, proud, and successful moments of your career and personal life.

Pivotal Regrets

Past success breeds future success. And building on strengths is the most direct path to making great decisions, increasing impact, and accelerating growth. But no one goes through life untouched by obstacles and disappointments. No one escapes at least some amount of regret: derailed projects, relationships gone wrong, hiring disasters, or promotions that didn't materialize.

Sometimes our disappointments are minor. At other times, they're a really big deal. They're what I call Pivotal Regrets.

Though we may try to forget or ignore our regrets, there's no benefit to putting our heads in the sand. Though we may wish to, we can't simply dismiss our losses: our worst decisions, personal and professional shortcomings, missed opportunities, and outright failures. These Pivotal Regrets are part of what make us who we are—as people, as leaders. And sometimes they hold us back. Sometimes. But not always.

In fact, our negative experiences can be downright transformative. True growth lies in recognizing, facing, and learning from them.

Several years ago, I worked with Dana, a talented executive with a passion for improving outcomes and increasing staff engagement. She had been hand-picked for the role of COO by her former manager, Janet. Now CEO of a different organization, Janet recognized the tremendous value Dana had to offer. She personally invited Dana to join her leadership team at the new organization.

Being recruited for this role was one of Dana's proudest moments—a Pivotal Success. She gladly accepted the offer. In her new role, she worked closely with Janet. Together, they took the organization to a whole new level of industry recognition, employee engagement, customer service, and profitability.

Things changed for Dana when Janet was recruited to yet another company, leaving her without her main champion. She now had to navigate the organization's politics on her own as she simultaneously had to build a strong relationship with the incoming CEO. It wasn't easy for Dana, who didn't care to bring attention to herself or step on toes. She grew quiet in the face of dissenting opinions, took a back seat in meetings, and struggled to connect with her new boss. Within a year, she found herself pushed to the sidelines. As her influence waned, she realized it was time to move on.

Looking back, Dana regrets not taking a more confident stance. Had she been more vocal in the face of complex organizational dynamics and tough personalities, she might have secured support from other stakeholders and formed a connection with her new manager. As it turned out, she'd missed the opportunity. She lost ground and there was no going back.

In taking the time to reflect on that "debacle" (her words), Dana gained insight that will guide future decisions. She is determined to be bolder and more outspoken as she approaches future opportunities.

Now let's focus on you. Take a look at the following list of Pivotal Regrets. They are examples of regrets identified by some of my most accomplished clients. See which of these may reflect your own life experience. Be sure to think about your unique path, reflecting on key disappointments, losses, challenges, and regrets.

- *Accepted the first job offer that came along*
- *Took on a dead-end assignment*
- *Left a job on poor terms (burning bridges)*
- *Ignored your true calling or passion*
- *Opted out of an MBA or other degree*
- *Took a job or promotion that didn't suit your strengths*
- *Became estranged from colleagues, friends, or family members*
- *Passed on a great investment*
- *Implemented a poor strategy*
- *Alienated peers, boss, direct reports, or members of the Board*
- *Developed counter-productive habits*
- *Failed to gather support for your agenda*
- *Struggled with a failing relationship*
- *Received a life changing diagnosis*
- *Lost a loved one*

Pivotal Regrets	Impact
_____	_____
_____	_____
_____	_____
_____	_____
_____	_____

Remember, this isn't the time to gloss over your losses, poor decisions, and missed opportunities. Be honest about challenges faced and mistakes made. Don't berate yourself or become mired in the struggles of the past. But do take a courageous look in the rearview mirror. And know this. Adversity can be a tremendous catalyst for change.

Take some time to consider:

- *How have your Pivotal Regrets helped you become a better leader, stronger person, wiser mentor, or more reliable colleague?*
- *How have you used your failures as motivation to get up and try something new, different, and more effective?*
- *Which insights can you glean from past mistakes?*
- *How can you use past challenges or obstacles as a catalyst for change?*
- *How will you approach your current role and responsibilities differently and to greater effect, given your prior setbacks?*
- *What can you teach others based on the difficulties you've faced and trials you've overcome?*

Here are three of my personal disappointments, missed opportunities, and losses.

My Pivot Points: Pivotal Regrets

Pivotal regret	Impact
Went directly from college to grad school	Didn't take time to pursue my love of travel or follow my dream of living abroad. Lesson: I now recognize the value of taking a pause and a detour along life's path. There's no rush, and taking a side route can be incredibly enriching.
Turned down PhD scholarship offer at UVA	I didn't recognize the long-term impact or the amazing opportunities UVA had to offer. Lesson: I use this to encourage my children to make wise choices about school, life, and career, weighing multiple factors. I also now remind myself not to pass up the extraordinary opportunities that come my way!
Lost my father to cancer, 67 years old	I still miss my dad every day. He would have been thrilled to know my children as they grow up, he would have been very proud of the work I do—and he'd have loved to be reading this very book. Lesson: Appreciate the important people in your life. When you lose a loved one, it's more than okay to take a pause to mourn the loss. Use their memory to become even stronger and more determined to live life and make a meaningful contribution to the world.

CHAPTER 4

Setting Your Sights

What Do You Love, What Do You Bring, and Where Are You Headed?

Now that you've examined your past, let's turn to the present. You've reviewed the myriad influences that brought you to this point. This is the perfect time to evaluate some important questions about who you are, what you bring, where you're headed, and what's holding you back. See Chapter 8 for worksheets to help you structure your reflections. Consider the following:

- *Who am I today: As a leader, mentor, colleague, business partner, etc.?*
- *What do I bring? What are my signature strengths and talents?*
- *Am I currently putting my strengths to use and doing the kind of work I love?*
- *Am I adding value in ways that mean the most to me?*
- *Where am I heading? Am I going in the best possible direction?*
- *Am I truly thriving—or just getting by?*

As a leader, you should also assess your organization. You can do this in quiet reflection, a great reason to take a strategic pause. You can gain further insight by asking key colleagues and customers for feedback. You can engage your team in the dialogue. In fact, the most valuable approach is to gain a variety of perspectives on the following:

- *Who are we today, as a team and company?*
- *What do we bring? What are our signature strengths and talents?*
- *Are we putting our strengths to use and doing the kind of work we love?*

- *Are we adding value in ways that mean the most to us, the company, our customers, clients and industry?*
- *Where are we heading? Are we positioned to create the best possible outcomes now and in the year(s) ahead?*
- *Are we truly thriving—or just getting by?*

Another consideration: *Am I (are we) operating in a way that aligns with our values?* This is incredibly important, so take your time to thoughtfully reflect on this following:

- *What do I (we) value most deeply, and what are my (our) greatest motivations?*
  - *Commercial success/revenue/income/wealth*
  - *Power*
  - *Recognition*
  - *Innovation*
  - *Building something from the bottom up*
  - *Fixing something that's broken (turnaround)*
  - *Sustaining success*
  - *Protecting the environment (sustainability)*
  - *Creating the future*
  - *Making a meaningful contribution to company, customers, patients, colleagues, industry, family, friends, community, environment, world, etc.*

Debbie Visconi, CEO, Bergen Regional Medical Center, had this to say about the importance of focusing on values:

Health care leaders tend to focus on the immediate needs to transform the business, whether it is to focus on the bottom line or in growing market share. We sometimes forget about the basics, our reason for being. When I was at Beth Israel Medical Center, our president's directive was, "We've got to get back to the basics. Why are we really here? We're here take care of the patients and what's important to them." That directive helped us refocus and reprioritize the work we were doing. That's when we all slowed down to speed up.

What Do You Bring? What Do You Love?

As important as it is to identify and build on strengths, some of my clients need a bit of encouragement to reflect on the question of *What do I bring?* Some are often humble leaders who don't like to toot their own horns. Others are their own worst critics, who prefer focus on what can be improved (*What do I have to fix?*). They downplay their strengths, even when it's strengths that have helped them succeed. And so, I remind them (as I'm reminding you) "good-to-great" starts with good.

What's the good you bring? (See Chapter 8 for a worksheet to help you with this.)

- *amiable*
- *candid*
- *clear*
- *communicative*
- *considerate*
- *decisive*
- *diligent*
- *direct*
- *discerning*
- *flexible*
- *honest*
- *open*
- *strategic*
- *thoughtful*
- *transparent*
- *trustworthy*
- *visionary*

What you bring generally is, and ideally should be, aligned with what you love. Reflect on what you love to do.

- *advocating for your team*
- *conveying a compelling message*
- *crafting the strategy*

- *developing new business*
- *developing your team*
- *implementation (hands-on)*
- *interacting with customers/clients*
- *international travel*
- *managing a diverse team*
- *meeting with investors*
- *mentoring future leaders*
- *serving on boards*
- *setting the vision*
- *starting up a new business unit or company*
- *turning a business around*
- *winning in a competitive market*

The greatest success and satisfaction, for you and your organization, lies in aligning what you bring and what you love. Seek opportunities—in your company, with your current or new team, in a different role, new endeavor, or beyond the workplace—to increase impact, unleash creativity, increase revenue and enjoy life.

My client, Caroline, left her job when it was no longer fulfilling. She was frustrated by the organizational politics and endless roadblocks in her way. To identify a more rewarding opportunity, Caroline took the time to reflect on herself (*Who am I? What do I bring? What do I love?*) and her experiences (*Pivot Points*). She thought about her career path, leadership style, personal strengths, and passions. She astutely recognized that this sort of reflection would play a key role in finding the right place to land.

> For me, it's always been about being able to contribute to those who need you the most. Having an impact in your community and an impact on staff, that's always been exciting to me. Being able to mentor, lead, coach staff to get to the next level, or whatever level they want to get to, so that they can best support our patients and communities. To me, that's what's most exciting and interesting about being a senior leader—being able to grow those around me to the next level so they can support the community.

Turning an organization around is also very gratifying. If you're able to walk into an organization that's in trouble and turn things around, it is incredibly rewarding. That's what we do as mission-driven professionals. We want to help. We want to make things better. I think that's exciting.

Caroline took the time for an honest look in the mirror and thoughtfully considered what was most rewarding and important to her. As a results, she's in the best position ever to confidently articulate who she is: a mission-driven, empowering, action-oriented leader who gets things done.

What's Holding You Back?

When you're moving at breakneck speed, there's little time to reflect on the hurdles in your way. But if you (or your team or company) aren't as successful as you'd like, you absolutely must slow down to ask the question, *What's holding me back?*

Whether you're facing a leadership challenge (need to be more decisive, influential, strategic), personal hurdle (health concerns, marital problems, poor self-image), or business issue (new regulations, heavy competition, shrinking margins), there's little chance of improvement if you don't stop to examine the problem. Only then can you identify solutions and get to work—filling in the gaps, getting up to speed, setting the stage for a whole new level of success.

You can dig into this by reflecting on your Pivotal Regrets. Which of these has held you back? *What are the past events or influences that have slowed your progress? Which external obstacles stand in your way today? What are the internal barriers that stand in the way of success?* Here are some of the hurdles my clients have faced:

- *Family commitments/conflicts*
- *Fear of failure*
- *Health concerns*
- *Ineffective communication: Too detailed, abrupt, indirect, technical, abstract or formal*
- *Lack of confidence*

- *Lack of executive presence*
- *Lack of international experience*
- *Limited experience in a given role, function, or industry*
- *Limited network/connections*
- *No MBA or other advanced degree*
- *Perfectionism*
- *Reluctance to ask for help*
- *Reticence to overshadow a boss, peer, parent, sibling, etc.*
- *Slow to adapt to changing circumstances*

To thrive as a leader—and to lead your organization to a whole new level of success—you have to figure out what's holding you back. Be honest with yourself but don't become preoccupied with challenges or shortcomings. Instead, identify ways to leap over these hurdles as you sprint toward success. You can capture your thoughts in the worksheets provided in Chapter 8.

If You Don't Let Go, You Won't Move Forward

Paul is the founder and CEO of a legal outsourcing firm. He is a great attorney, well-spoken, and incredibly smart. To run a successful company, however, Paul must learn to lead and delegate. He's got to hire a competent team. He has to provide the vision and strategy, training and resources. And he's got to manage the high-level customer relationships to ensure repeat business, referrals, and continued growth.

Like many other founders, Paul finds it difficult to let go. He allows himself to get pulled into the details. He gets caught up in addressing conflict and fielding complaints from his team. He stays up late and rises early to deal with non-urgent issues and distractions. The result? He spends far too little time on customer relationships, vision, and strategy.

Paul's attachment to the work and reticence to step out of the details are holding him, and his company, back. His failure to have the team work things out independently is another impediment. As the leader of a global organization, he must drive cultural awareness, drive accountability and expect his employees to collaborate well. Until he begins to focus on what's most important: strategic leadership, great relationships and a compelling view of the future, his business will never reach its full potential.

You Just Can't Write a Book in a Night

In writing this book, I've had my share of starts and stops. The starts were great. Ideas came to mind. I wrote them down. Stories unfolded. I wrote them down. The book began to flow.

But then the stops came along. Writing became more difficult. At times, the words wouldn't come. Or they would, but they didn't look quite right on the page. The stories didn't always shine through the way I had imagined. My transitions sometimes felt clunky and awkward. If you've ever written a book—or a report, presentation, speech, or proposal—you probably know how this feels.

To make meaningful progress, I had to figure out what was getting in the way. What was stalling my creativity? What was holding me back?

In the mid-1980s, I was an undergrad at Cornell University. It was an exciting place to be, with interesting students from around the globe, challenging classes, and brilliant professors working at the cutting edge of research. The academic rigor was more demanding than anything I'd encountered in high school. I had to put more thought, time, and effort into everything I did.

Unfortunately, I'd brought along some bad habits from my high school years—such as my tendency to procrastinate. As a high school student, I would delay completing my assignments to the last possible minute. I remember staying up all night, clacking away on my electric typewriter, as the hours passed, and my eyes grew weary. Still, I was able to get the work done, dragging myself into school with a decent piece of work and without serious repercussion.

As a college student, although I could no longer complete an assignment in one night, my procrastination continued. I was aware of it and actually wrote my honors thesis on the topic. Somehow, even with the increased rigor of college, I managed to leave much of my work until I couldn't postpone another minute. As you can imagine, I had my share of long nights and tired days.

Fast forward to today and the writing of *Slow Down to Speed Up*. It didn't take long to realize: You can't write a book in a night.

As I started to write, I began much as I write my newsletters and articles: I opened my laptop and began hitting the keys. After all, I had long been formulating the key points. I'd developed a number of the concepts and activities; in fact, my clients were already using many of them. And so, the approach worked well for the first few months. I got my thoughts onto the page. I felt good about my progress.

Until suddenly, I lost momentum. The ideas crystallized less rapidly. I began to waste hours editing my work rather than adding new material. I allowed myself to obsess over words and phrase, stories and titles, making changes for no compelling reason.

I had become my own micromanager and critic, pouring wasted hours into minute adaptations of no material value.

The fact was, I had slowed down (truly!) but I wasn't speeding up.

I called upon my friend and confidante, Sarah. During a recent conversation with her, I had an aha! moment. I realized I was going about the writing process in a way that no was longer effective.

The process of opening my laptop, typing out ideas and self-editing might work for term papers and newsletters, but it is a lousy way to write a book.

Speaking with Sarah helped me realize that I needed to adapt in two key ways. I had to:

1. Stop working on my laptop. Take out a pad and pen, allow the ideas to flow, resist the temptation to change the wording, format, etc.
2. Spend more time talking about my ideas before putting them to paper. I accomplished this with media interviews, discussion with clients and colleagues, and "interviewing" myself (recording and transcribing along with way).

My point is this. While it may seem that these steps would slow me down, they actually helped me write the book far more quickly. If I hadn't adjusted my approach, I might not have gotten the book out into the world, and into your hands.

I've learned my own lesson. Sometimes you really do have to slow down, figure out what's holding you back, and adapt your approach.

Setting Your Sights: Where Are You Headed?

If you've worked on some of the activities in this book, you've begun the process of slowing down to speed up. Perhaps you are starting to feel more comfortable reflecting and taking the time to be proactive, strategic, and diligently focused on the long term.

If so, this is a great time to zero in on your vision. What does success actually look like? What's your pinnacle role, ideal business model or ultimate victory? Can you picture yourself reaching the dominant position in your market, transforming your industry, becoming the next CEO or Chairman of the Board? This may sound pie-in-the-sky but don't hold back from setting big goals. That's what vision is all out. Ask yourself: what does it mean to truly thrive? And what will it take to get there?

In today's busy, demanding world, taking the time to craft your vision can be a challenge. Developing a vision requires time and thoughtful reflection. It takes openness and insight. And none of that can happen effectively if you are rushing through your days, putting out fires or just trying to survive.

My client, Christopher, knows this challenge well. When I first met Chris, he was a mid-career marketing executive, working for a $50 billion company. Happily married, with two wonderful children and aging parents, Chris was doing well enough in life. He made a decent salary, enjoyed his work, loved his family, and could have continued on his current path without significant disruption. Still, Chris felt he was at a crossroads. He was effectively leading a small team but felt his leadership progression had slowed to a crawl. In his current role, there was little opportunity to advance. He knew he could add more and, if nothing changed, he would be ultimately unfulfilled.

To be clear, Chris had been doing great work. He received frequent compliments peers, manager, and clients. He led his team well and took a hands-on approach to the work.

Chris wanted more than that. He was increasingly eager for a larger leadership role. Yet, his tendency to dive into the work rather than delegating to his team meant he was chronically busy and often stretched thin. He found it increasingly difficult to balance the intense work demands with the desire to be an available father, spouse, and son for the family that loved him.

Chris had little time to crystallize what he truly wanted and develop a plan to get there. Lacking a clear vision, his role in the organization remained status quo. It was good enough for now but the desire to do more nagged at him, often just below the surface.

Like so many executives, Chris found himself caught up in the busyness of business. He spent long hours getting things done but took little time to reflect upon personal goals or long-term vision.

During the course of our work, Chris began to slow down. Using the framework I provided, he took a close look at where he'd been (Pivot Points), what he brought, what he loved, and what was holding him back. He reviewed where he was heading and he developed clarity about where he ultimately wanted to be.

Once his vision was clear, Chris began to identify how to achieve his goals. Using my *Accelerating Success Action Plan*, he pinpointed the actions that would expedite progress. He used this newfound clarity to move ahead with confidence and conviction. Chris decided to engage his manager in candid discussions about career path. As a result, they were able to identify the roles, skills, and experiences he would need to pursue.

Take the advice I gave Chris. Step out of the busyness. Reflect on your path. Develop your vision of success, for yourself, team, and company. Think beyond the next meeting, monthly deadlines, quarterly milestones, and annual goals. Look to the long term. Where do you want to be, and what do you want to achieve—in a year, 5 years, 10, or 20?

You won't be able to do this in a busy office, with phones ringing, people at your door, and distractions from every corner. Find a quiet place. If you are at work, seek out a little-used conference room to avoid unwanted interruptions. Or head to the local coffee shop for a bit of distance and fewer workplace distractions. Go to a park, hotel lobby, or bookstore. Any quiet location will do.

Once you've found your ideal reflection spot, eliminate distractions. Put away your phone. Turn off the notifications on your laptop. Stay away from e-mail. Take a deep breath and relax.

Now conjure up an image of your future self: content, fulfilled, and remarkably successful. You can also reflect on your team or organization. Imagine you've transformed your industry, developed an extraordinary way to improve people's lives, created a breakthrough process that elevates your company to a whole new level. Take your time and answer the following:

- *What are you doing, thinking, and feeling in this vision?*
- *What accounts for your increased success, confidence, and satisfaction?*
- *How have you improved your approach to leadership or the achievement of your goals?*
- *How does your future self make outstanding decisions, drive strategy, take meaningful action, or develop a new generation of leaders?*
- *What's your future team doing especially well?*
- *How has your company transformed the competitive landscape?*

Make your vision as vivid as possible and don't hold back. Review your vision monthly, quarterly, or annually. Discuss your ideas with a trusted colleague, mentor, manager, or your leadership team. Think big, project forward, and start to formulate an actionable plan. Consider the following:

- *To achieve your vision of the future, what do you need to do immediately?*
- *What needs to happen in the next week, month, quarter, or year?*
- *What must you do today to succeed tomorrow?*

Turn to Chapter 8 for a worksheet to help you capture your ideal future state and lay the groundwork for getting there.

PART TWO

Speed Up!

Newly armed with self-insight, confidently knowing who you are, what you bring, and where you're going, you are ready to hit the ground running. It's time to use your thoughtful reflections to map the path forward. Using the *Accelerating Success Action Plan (ASAP)* in Chapter 7, you will be able to dramatically expedite your results. You will also have the tools you need to help your team achieve better, faster results, increase innovation, quickly arrive at key milestones (minus the mistakes that have slowed or derailed past efforts), accelerate growth, and enhance industry repute. The possibilities are limitless.

CHAPTER 5

Taking the Wheel

Do the Right Things, Make the Best Decisions, Master Time

To succeed in today's 24/7 world, leaders must focus on the right things, spend time in the right ways, make thoughtful decisions, and recognize where to let go. Yet as the pace of business accelerates and the demand for quick results intensifies, many leaders feel pressure to do more than ever, assume personal ownership for work that should be handled by others, put in unreasonably long hours, and relinquish control of their personal time.

It is not a sustainable model and it's no way to thrive. Truly effective leaders take the wheel and actively reclaim control. Here's how.

First Things First: Mastering the Prioritization Challenge

Leaders like you have an extraordinary amount to accomplish. There is ever more to be done than time in which to do it. It is a challenge to align pressing tasks with strategic priorities. Yet if you're constantly focused on the urgent, you will get pulled away from what's truly important.

I recently worked with Andrew, an executive with a monumental workload. He often worked 14 hours a day. He worked on weekends, too, and rarely took time to wind down. He spent too little with family, and the time he spent with them was punctuated by frequent calls, texts and e-mails. Andrew was becoming resentful. A compassionate leader, Andrew was also concerned about the stress on his overworked team. He spent a great deal of time sorting through the myriad demands that came at them, many of which were portrayed as high priority. Lacking clarity on where to devote time and energy, he was overwhelmed and frustrated. It was impossible to please everyone.

Andrew was a high achiever and a hard worker, but even he couldn't master the sheer volume of work. If he didn't learn to distinguish the most important activities from those that could wait, he would soon fail on multiple fronts.

He had to learn to prioritize, and fast.

The prioritization challenge may be familiar to you. When everything feels urgent, you spread yourself thin to get it all done. You begin to feel stretched and overwhelmed. Your approach may become fragmented or reactive. You go through your days putting out fires and lose sight of strategic priorities. Creativity and productivity decline.

While you can survive like this for a while, ultimately you will fall short. You will lose steam and your reputation will take a hit. This is no way to thrive.

Do you remember my client, Dianne? When we first began our work, Dianne was in jeopardy of damaging her stellar reputation. She was chronically behind in her work. She was late to meetings. She missed deadlines. And it was really catching up to her.

In discussing a large potential project, one of her clients told her, "Dianne, I know you're the one to do this work. But frankly, I'm worried. You're always behind schedule and we can't afford delays." Disturbing as it was to hear, Diane valued the feedback. It was a wake-up call. She and I began to work immediately on improving prioritization, to help her take charge of her time and save her reputation. As a result, Dianne was able to reassure the client, regain her momentum, and win a contract for major new piece of work.

Although Dianne and Andrew faced different challenges, and worked in vastly different environments, they both needed to master the prioritization challenge. As they learned to slow down and reflect on what was most important, they began to master time, effort, and energy. They became more effective leaders. They felt less overwhelmed. They consistently delivered on crucial commitments. And they freed up time to strategize, influence, and create future success.

Here are five questions you can use to identify priorities (and set aside subordinate or peripheral activities). Take your time, think about it. Then rate each item on your "to do" list per the scale, below.

Priority Assessment Tool

1. *Does this activity align with my strategy?* _____
2. *Does this activity directly advance my top goals?* _____
3. *Does my manager/client/colleague agree that it is a top priority item?* _____
4. *Does this activity add significant value?* _____
5. *How pressing is the deadline?* _____

Scoring:

1 = no/not at all, 3 = somewhat, 5 = yes/very

- An activity receiving a score of 4 or 5 on *three to five* of the above questions is a *top* priority.
- An activity receiving a score of 4 or 5 on *one or two* of the above questions is a priority.
- Everything else is subordinate and should be treated accordingly. You may choose to delay action, delegate to someone else, or take it off your radar entirely.

If you aren't being sufficiently thoughtful and strategic in the way you handle your workload, it's only a matter of time before the demands get the better of you. Prioritize as if your job or business relies on it. The fact is, it does.

CIA: Control, Influence, Accept/Adapt

A lack of control can be extremely frustrating for any leader. Yet there are often variables over which a leader has little or no control. Do any of these ring a bell?

- *There is a hiring freeze and you can't extend an offer to a stellar candidate.*
- *Your boss is retiring and now you must adapt to the style of a more difficult manager.*

- *The stock market is down and investors are worried.*
- *Your new product fails to gain regulatory approval.*
- *Your top performer is leaving the company.*
- *The company gets acquired by a larger corporate entity and the rules of the game change—a lot.*

The list goes on and on. As challenging as these situations are, they can take up a disproportionate amount of a leader's time, attention, and emotional bandwidth. Executives are accustomed to having influence and, in many cases, direct control. When that goes out the window, it can be disruptive and distracting.

To avoid wasting time and energy trying to control the uncontrollable, I advise my clients to reflect on what's happening in their business (and life) through the lens of *CIA: Control, Influence, Accept/Adapt.* It's a straightforward framework for making decisions—quickly, efficiently, and without undue stress or wasted energy. The next time you are faced with an important decision, ask yourself:

- *Is this a situation or decision over which I have direct control? If so, how will I exert that control and what outcome do I want to achieve?*
- *If I don't have direct control, can I influence the decision or outcome? If so, how can I most effectively exert that influence?*
- *If I have neither control nor influence, can I accept the situation? It may not be my preference but it's the reality. What can I do, in that case, to make it more palatable, comfortable, positive, and successful? What must I do to adapt? And if I can't accept or adapt . . . what then?*

Henry, a Fortune 100 executive, successfully used my CIA framework to deal with a stressful situation. Henry had recently been offered a promotion to a new role, in which he'd interact closely with top company leaders. It was a very exciting opportunity. The role was ideally suited to his diverse skillset. It would allow him to materially impact the company's performance and reputation. He was anxious to get started.

Unfortunately for Henry, there was an unforeseen obstacle in his path. Just days after he'd received the verbal offer, word of the new role made its way up to the C-suite, where organizational dynamics took over.

His promotion was stalled by a top executive, who froze the process until further notice.

As you can imagine, Henry was displeased. In his eyes, he'd been shortchanged by the company to which he'd devoted the past 15 years of his career. He felt confused and angry. He began to question whether the organization truly valued him. He also wondered whether his manager had left him out to dry. His typical enthusiasm began to wane in the face of this deep disappointment.

Henry felt he had a decision to make. But he wasn't quite sure how to make it. So we worked within the CIA framework, to help him gain clarity and move forward with confidence. I advised Henry to ask himself:

C: Do I have control over the freezing of his promotion?
I: Can I influence the situation?
A: If need be, can I accept or adapt?

Using the CIA framework, Henry recognized that no, he did not have direct control. The decision was now in the hands of management. He had already tried to exert influence, talking to his manager and other stakeholders who might be able to champion his cause. None of them was willing or able to intervene. And so, he would have to decide: Could he accept the situation and deal with the disappointment? Would he be able to adapt to the more limited parameters of his current mandate? Or, if unable to accept and unwilling to adapt, what different path should he choose?

Upon reflection, Henry concluded that he didn't want to leave his company. He loved his work and he knew he was making a difference in the lives of his customers. He respected his manager and appreciated the autonomy and flexibility of his position. So, he decided to sit tight, put his best foot forward, and wait for the promotion to unfold over time. By accepting this turn of events and adapting to the disappointment he'd felt, Henry was able to let go. The weight of anger and frustration lifted. His typically upbeat mood and energy returned. And he began, once again, to feel excited and energized by his work.

As a leader, it is essential to recognize what you control and what you don't. If you are at the helm of a team or organization, you do have direct control over a great many things. But let's be clear: even when you have direct control, it rarely works to be excessively controlling. In most business contexts, decision-making is no longer a matter of command and control. A more effective approach could be called contextualize and convince.

Here's what Jeff Moody, former CEO of Rita's Italian Ice and Subway Franchise Advertising Fund Trust, had to say:

> Even when you, as the leader, have decision-making authority, you've got to convince others of your point of view. Too many leaders go straight to control and make the direct decisions. But if you first try to convince the other folks of the wisdom of your point of view, it's easier to bring them along willingly. If you can't convince them, and after listening to everybody's argument, you still believe that you ultimately have accountability for the decision, then you make the decision. You take control. And everyone has to get on board.

Start Saying No!

If you're like many of my clients, you probably find it easier to say yes than no. After all, you like to help. You want to be part of the solution. You enjoy the opportunity to demonstrate your abundant energy and your readiness to support the company.

Requests from above, including your boss or dotted-line supervisors, can be harder to decline than others. And if you are customer-focused, you may not wish to refuse client requests, even when those requests are unreasonable, poorly timed, unfair, or ill-conceived. If you are especially collaborative, you may find it difficult to say no to a peer or business partner. Or, if you are in the C-Suite, you may find yourself saying yes to the Board, occasionally against your better judgment, at the expense of other priorities, or at the risk of organizational disruption. Politics play a major role at this level, and it can be tough to say no.

Still, there are times when you must decline, or at least defer, the demands that come at you. There are only so many hours in a day, so many days each week. Every time you say yes, you reduce time for other activities, many of which are quite important.

By strategically saying no, you free up time to:

- Identify new ways to help customers and clients
- Accelerate progress
- Beat a deadline
- Meet with important stakeholders/engage your constituents
- Bring your team together: To build relationships, improve communication, increase collaboration, align around priorities
- Relax and recharge (pause, take a walk, eat your lunch)
- Take a more strategic approach
- Diffuse a situation before it explodes
- Hone your vision
- Go to an industry event/sit on a panel/network
- Mentor a young employee
- Get home a little earlier (have dinner with family, attend your child's sporting event, musical performance, or teacher conference)
- Build your brand as a proactive leader who thoughtfully applies time and energy to getting the right things done

So before you reflexively agree to a request or dive into an activity, ask yourself: Is this activity best accomplished by me personally or can/should it go to someone else?

Me/Not Me

The fact is, some activities are your direct responsibility. They belong to you. Matters of strategy, influence, vision, and communication are good examples of where a leader must take an active role. On the other hand, a thriving leader can't allow himself to continually get pulled into the details or bogged down by day-to-day execution. Some things simply must be delegated.

You may worry about burdening your team with additional work. But make no mistake, it is your responsibility to develop them, provide stretch opportunities, increase their visibility, and develop successors. By delegating work and empowering your team to make decisions, you create a win for everyone.

As Trish O'Keefe progressed along her leadership path, starting as a bedside nurse and culminating in her recent promotion to Morristown Memorial Medical Center president, she had to learn to let go. She had to put day-to-day operations into the hands of her leadership team and the hundreds of dedicated employees throughout the organization. Here's what she told me about that:

> Sometimes it's so much easier just do the work, but it's better to frame an objective and let people learn, evolve and make mistakes. And then support them when they need you to. You think you can do all and be all, but you can't. You need to really step back and take the time to think about, *Okay, how can I support these people and allow them to grow as well?*

If you're not the right person for a given task or activity, give it to someone else. But who is the right person for the job? Ask the following:

If Not Me, Who?

- *Who has capacity for the work, or an interest in the current opportunity?*
- *Is this work something I can delegate to a direct report, providing her with the opportunity to stretch, learn, and gain recognition?*
- *Is this request best directed to a different department or team? (Be thoughtful here. You don't want to be viewed as a leader who passes the buck. So be sure you give a heads-up to the person or team to whom you've directed the request.)*

And if you've come to recognize that you really are the right person for a given activity, you still need to determine how quickly to get to it. Here's how.

Now/Later/Never

The fact is, some things really do have to be addressed without delay. Those are usually easy to spot. Here are a few examples:

- *The FDA is coming to investigate a product, process, or complaint. You must be prepared; there's no wiggle room.*
- *A client has a valid emergency and needs your attention by the end of the day.*
- *There is a major announcement impacting your company's public image, industry standing or stock price; you need to issue a statement to get out ahead of the storm.*

Less urgent activities and requests can sometimes be deferred. Still others can be declined, to preserve time for higher impact actions and more pressing demands. That sometimes means turning down good opportunities as you create space for the great ones.

Step back periodically to review your pending tasks and activities. Slow down and thoughtfully review each new opportunity and request that comes along. Decide : *Am I going to say yes or no?* If you say yes, will you move it to the front of the queue? Or defer while you attend to more pressing matters? The following questions will help you decide:

- *Is this (really) a priority item? (see Priority Assessment Tool)*
- *Is it time-sensitive?*
- *Is it better to defer until some preliminary steps have been taken?*
- *Is it better postponed until we've reached the next milestone on a key project (to avoid missing a deadline)?*
- *Is this action or initiative likely to have better funding or support if I postpone to next quarter, year, or later?*

If you decide to say no to a specific task or request—assuming you've paused to consider whether this is the right time, place, and reason— you'll need some diplomatic language at your disposal. Your words need to be thoughtful, authentic, and credible. They should be considerate of the other person's best interests. Here are a few of the many ways to thoughtfully say *no, later,* or *not me*:

How to Diplomatically Defer, Decline, or Deflect

- *"If this can wait 2 weeks, I can give you my full attention at that time."*
- *"Of course, I'd be happy to help. Let me connect you to Joe, who has the capacity and expertise to do this right away."*
- *"I can do this for you right away if we pause on your other project/ request. Which is your top priority?"*
- *"I would love to help but the team is under the gun on another project. I don't want you to get short shrift. May I help connect you to another resource?"*
- *"What do you need to achieve, and how quickly? Let me help you find a way to meet that objective even more rapidly."*

Targeted E-mail Response System: TERS

In today's business world, an intense reliance on e-mail is nearly universal. It is often the primary avenue of communication. And that can be a problem. After all, e-mail is often not the best way to convey ideas, drive collaboration or build solid partnerships. Tone can be difficult to convey and misunderstandings are common. E-mail is also an enormous theft of an executive's time.

It may feel that e-mail has been in our lives forever; but, of course, it hasn't.

In the early 90s, I was a graduate student working toward my PhD in clinical psychology. While I'd yet to begin my dissertation, the program required that we engage in research. And so, when one of my professors invited me to assist with a project she was co-leading with a colleague in Germany, I was excited to jump in. I liked this professor, was interested in her topic of study, and loved the idea of working across cultures.

The work required frequent interaction with the German research group. Of course, by today's lens, that sounds straightforward. After all, we live and work in a world of e-mail, texts, and video conferences. But in 1991, the technology wasn't even close to what it is today. This was pre-AOL and its familiar alert: "You've got mail."

The US and German researchers could interact by phone but that posed challenges. There was a 5-hour time zone difference, for one thing. And the telephone offered limited opportunity to share research data. It was simply an inadequate way to work together.

Fortunately, my professor and her colleague had university affiliations that allowed them to connect by computer. And so, as I began to participate in the project, I gained my first introduction to the amazing world of e-mail. It was an efficient form of communication and I rapidly came to rely upon it.

Fast forward to today. Do you remember my client, Mark, the executive who spent 2 hours a day clearing his inbox before the sun came up? Mark was overwhelmed by the volume of e-mail to review. He preferred to take a first pass at his inbox before getting to work, to preserve time for the myriad other, higher priority, activities. Of course, he knew well that the e-mails would continue to arrive all day and into the evening. His morning e-mail regimen was merely an attempt to get ahead of the tsunami.

It wasn't long before Mark's lack of sleep caught up with him. His patience began to thin, his concentration suffered, and his ability to make quick, strategic decisions took a hit. He couldn't go on like this forever.

So I gave Mark a method to rapidly reduce e-mail overwhelm. Almost immediately, his focus improved and he began to be more patient with his team and colleagues. He had greater energy. And he became far more resilient in the face of daily challenges and the stressors of the job.

There are two main components to my TERS system. You'll need just a little time to set it up. Trust me, this kind of pause in the daily flood of activity will pay off. You will gain more time for more strategic pursuits, greater energy and focus, and maybe even an extra couple hours' sleep. Here's how it works.

1. Ask for a Headline

Talk to your team, colleagues, anybody from whom you receive e-mail. Tell them you are trying to be more efficient with your time and more effective in the way you respond to communications. Ask them to start the subject line of any e-mail message with one of three headlines:

ACTION: *Immediate action/decision*
FYI: *For your information*
TALK: *Let's talk*

While **ACTION** may seem self-explanatory, you must align with others on what actually constitutes an immediate need. Chances are, there will be plenty of actions that others consider urgent but you don't, and vice-versa. Have the upfront discussion to create mutual understanding, prevent confusion, and avoid wasted time.

FYI e-mails abound in corporate America but many of these are a waste of a leader's valuable time. Ask to be taken off group e-mails and lengthy threads unless it is essential that you see the exchange of information. Ideally, e-mails should be short, to the point, and sent only when truly needed.

TALK is my personal favorite. The reality is, most of our communication can be effectively handled with a quick discussion by phone or in person. My client, Renee, agrees. She told me:

> So much time gets wasted by carrying on discussions by e-mail instead of picking up a phone. It takes at least twice as long to get a resolution by e-mail. Even if I give the first two minutes of a given phone call to saying 'Hello, how are you?' it still takes longer by e-mail to move right to the issue.

2. Set clear Parameters

Decide how often you will check your e-mail. Many of my clients continually check e-mail throughout the day. They allow notifications to continually disrupt them, even when they are in meetings. It is not an effective approach.

Before Mary adopted my Targeted E-mail Reduction System, she struggled with the impulse to check her inbox morning through night. But she knew something would have to change to free herself of e-mail overwhelm. So she decided to give TERS a try. Instead of getting up before sunrise and being e-mail accessible all day long, she decided to checked her inbox five times a day: from home at 6 a.m., from work at 10 a.m., 1 p.m. and 4:30 p.m., and once more at home in the evening. This gave her peace of mind, knowing she'd catch anything truly pressing, while freeing up time for other matters. Without the constant distraction of e-mail, Mary could truly focus on learning her new role, developing relationships with important stakeholders, scoring some early wins, and crafting her strategic imperatives.

If you are concerned that you'll miss time-sensitive messages or appear unavailable when needed, trust me, you're not alone. I hear frequently from my clients, many of whom feel like virtual slaves to their e-mail. The solution lies in setting clear parameters and having an emergency contact method, the proverbial Batphone. Give your manager, team, colleagues, and clients a way to reach you for urgent matters. They can call your mobile phone, text you, contact your assistant, or send an instant message. Just be sure you've developed clarity and mutual agreement around what is genuinely urgent.

Stakeholder Priority Plan

My client, Ron, recently received a promotion. As Senior Vice President, he now has a seat at the table with top executives in his company, many of whom had formerly been several organizational layers above him. To be successful, he'll have to establish a new kind of relationship with them, in which he will be a peer rather than a subordinate. He'll also have to establish a line of communication and a strong partnership with an array of other stakeholders: new peers, manager, and leadership team.

A principle challenge is the sheer number of relationships to work on. Each of Ron's stakeholders has a distinct agenda, personal style, and organizational perspective. Each has unique preferences around communicating, collaborating, and making key decisions. Ron must create a tailored approach to optimizing each of these relationships.

Ron needs a plan, one that guides him to developing his most important stakeholder relationships first, and fast. He has but limited time to put his best foot forward. The fact is, people form first impressions quickly,

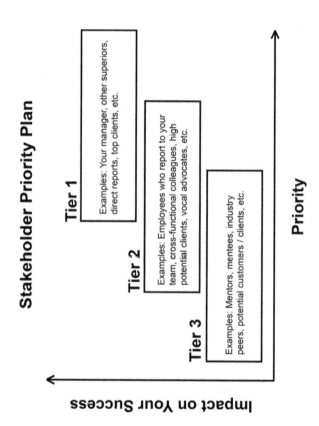

and those impressions tend to stick. Even the people who already know Ron are expecting changes in the relationship given his change in role.

So Ron and I recently got to work. I asked him to write down the name of each of his stakeholders. From there, he will assign priority categories and create a plan of action.

To develop your own Stakeholder Priority Plan, think about all of the stakeholders relevant to your success (in your business, a new role, or a personal or professional transition). Assign each to tier one, two or three.

Tier one stakeholders are your most important,. They can accelerate, slow or derail your success. Their support will help you rapidly progress. Their opposition can create major headaches. They are people of influence and power. They are the people with whom you must closely align to move your agenda forward.

Tier one stakeholders may include your manager, his or her manager and peers, your closest colleagues and leadership team. If you are the CEO, tier one includes members of the board. Important customers and clients are tier one. And if you deal with investors, media, or regulatory agencies, those relationships are tier one too.

Tier two stakeholders are a moderately lower priority but still important. They are people you must influence and with whom you must have a trusting relationship. However, the urgency to do so is less intense.

Tier two stakeholders may include the people who work for your direct reports. They may be colleagues in other functional areas with whom you need to collaborate but with whom you and your team interact less frequently. Some of your customers and clients will fall into this category too.

Tier three consists of everyone else. With a finite amount of time, tier one and two get first dibs on your attention, but tier three should not be ignored or dismissed. You don't want to miss out on a great idea from front line staff. You do need to inspire and engage the entire organization. And you never know when a small client account may turn into something big, so don't neglect your tier three customers.

Here's a template you can use for mapping out your Stakeholder Priority Plan. Keep it close at hand, as your relationships will have a tremendous impact on your level of success.

Once you've assigned a category to each stakeholder, you'll need to develop a plan to engage them. Consider:

- *Where, when, and how often will you meet?*
- *How formal or informal, scheduled or ad hoc?*
- *Will they be 1:1, in small groups, at a Town Hall?*
- *How quickly must you arrange time to meet?*
- *How can you build upon the strength of the existing relationship?*
- *Are there problems that must be fixed?*
- *What has to happen to rapidly create trust, improve communication, address conflict, or accelerate collaboration?*

Turn to Chapter 8 for a blank SPP template and worksheet.

CHAPTER 6

Relax, Recharge, Refuel

You Can't Thrive If You Are Running on Empty

There's no getting around it. Being a leader takes a tremendous amount of energy, stamina, and focus. It's not for the faint of heart. Remember the thousands of decisions you make each day, and the cognitive fatigue generated by all that decision-making? You will have to stay energized and clear-headed to make the kinds of decisions that help you, your team, and organization thrive.

Beyond that, you have to build stellar relationships with customers, business partners, managers and the board. You must develop a winning strategy, articulate your vision, guide the team, develop leaders, grow the business, inspire and influence your workforce. You have to navigate complexity, deal with organizational politics, create context, and develop a culture of excellence.

All of that is just on the business side of life. We haven't even talked about your responsibilities outside the office: family life, community leadership, spiritual life, philanthropic pursuits, and more.

Like all of my clients, you probably love to lead and you gain energy from the work itself. You thrive in building an exceptional team, growing market share, igniting creativity, inspiring a workforce, helping customers, driving innovation, and making a meaningful difference. You have a passion for leadership. It is your calling.

But let's be honest. Under the profound stress and pressure of today's fast-paced business environment, you can't thrive if you don't find a way to recharge and refuel. Stamina is a requirement of leadership and no one has an unlimited supply. Energy must be consistently replenished and renewed.

In this chapter, I will share with you the advice and tools I provide to clients across the Fortune 500. These techniques help them to remain healthy, energized, focused, and effective. They can do the same for you.

Put on Your Oxygen Mask

Several years ago, I was introduced to Kelly. A highly successful executive with an entrepreneurial background, Kelly has taken on an array of ventures and responsibilities. At every turn, she has established herself as a visionary thinker with a strategic mind and bright view of the future.

When we started working together, she was in the midst of a challenge. For months, she'd been trying to create support and alignment among her colleagues, a seasoned group of leaders with strong personalities, deep-seated opinions, and a history of unresolved conflicts.

Kelly's manager expected her to drive collaboration among this discordant group, to help increase innovation and elevate sales. Unfortunately, her colleagues seemed to fight her at every turn.

To the outside observer, Kelly looked calm despite the pressure. But on the inside, she was struggling. She often turned to the quick but temporary comfort of junk food. She stopped exercising. She ate lavish dinners with clients and colleagues during frequent travels across the globe. She struggled with sleep, waking up throughout the night as she reworked the events and difficulties of the day.

Kelly's poor eating habits, lack of exercise, and disrupted sleep led her to gain 40 pounds in less than 2 years. The extra weight exacerbated her inactivity and troubled sleep. Beyond that, her boss and peers started to worry about her health. They wondered whether she could handle the additional pressures of a pending promotion. They began to seriously rethink her readiness for the role.

Kelly didn't want to acknowledge—to her boss, herself, or anyone else—the severity of the problem. She told me all she really wanted was to have an impact, help the company grow, and support her team of high performers. And so, she continually put the needs of the company, customers, and team over her own. The overeating persisted, along with her feelings of frustration. Sleep remained elusive and her overall fitness declined. She was caught in a destructive loop—one that took a toll on her health, home life, leadership impact, and opportunity to grow.

My first challenge with Kelly was to help her slow down and acknowledge the problem. Given her strong work ethic and others-first mindset, this was no easy task. Yet for her situation to improve, she'd have to see that taking care of herself was neither self-indulgent nor optional.

I got through to Kelly with the analogy of putting on her own oxygen mask. Think of the announcements you hear at the outset of a flight. The flight attendants instruct you to "put on your own oxygen mask before helping others." And with good reason. If you run out of oxygen, you're going to pass out. You won't be able to help yourself or anyone else. On the contrary, someone will have to come help you, assuming you're fortunate enough to get their attention.

As a leader, it's your job to help others. But take my word for it; if you chronically neglect yourself, you will pay a price. As will your team, colleagues, customers, and family. There's simply no good outcome to running yourself down, disregarding your need for good nutrition, restful sleep, exercise, and relaxation.

You've got to put on your oxygen mask.

When Kelly embraced the idea that taking care of herself made her a more effective leader (not to mention, a better mother, spouse, and friend), she developed a plan that incorporated healthy eating, a daily fitness schedule, yoga, and nightly meditation for reduced stress and better sleep. In less than a year, she'd lost 30 pounds. Her sleep improved dramatically and she began to feel calmer and more resilient. Her manager's confidence increased, too, and Kelly received her coveted promotion.

If you're like Kelly, you tend to put others' needs ahead of your own. You take little time to care for yourself and perhaps it's starting to take a toll. Remember, the successful leader must find ways to unwind and recharge, to sleep and eat well, exercise consistently, and spend time with family and friends.

Here are some ways you can refill your tank, fueling mind and body, so you can be a remarkably energized, focused, effective leader.

Sleep Well

Think of sleep as the foundation. If the foundation of a home is crumbling, the house will fall soon enough. The same principle applies to us. Skip too much sleep and we, too, will fall.

It has been estimated that up to 70 percent of Americans have some sort of sleep disorder. In the developing world, there are approximately 150 million adults suffering from sleep difficulties.

If you aren't sleeping consistently and soundly, talk to your doctor. Identify, treat, or rule out any medical concerns. And consider one or more of the following remedies:

- Daily/nightly meditation. (There is a vast array of apps, classes, books, videos and guides to help you.)
- Herbal supplements and teas. (Consult with a doctor or nutritionist for targeted advice.)
- Do some yoga before bed.
- Create a calming sleep environment. (No electronic devices in the bedroom, no screen time for at least an hour before bed, sleep in a darkened, quiet room, keep the air cool but not cold.)
- Set up relaxing evening routines. (Take a warm bath, listen to calming music, enjoy some leisure reading. Remember, this is not the time for e-mails, Facebook, or binge watching your favorite shows on Netflix.)
- Limit or eliminate caffeine and alcohol, particularly in the evening hours.

Eat Well

- Eat whole foods and minimize or eliminate processed foods.
- Reduce sugars/sweets.
- Avoid fast foods.
- Stay hydrated throughout the day.
- Increase ready access to healthy foods. (Have your groceries/meals delivered.)
- Limit or eliminate caffeine and alcohol.

Stress Less

- Meditate daily. Even 10 minutes can have a meaningful impact.
- Do yoga. (Take a class, use an app, watch a video.)
- Exercise regularly. (Go to the gym, work with a trainer, ride your bike, train for a marathon . . . Find what you love and do it.)
- Take walks. (One idea: Get outside for a walking meeting.)
- Enjoy time at the beach, in the mountains, on a lake, in nature.
- Spend time with a pet. (Walk the dog, pet the cat.)
- Take up a hobby. (Drawing, painting, model trains, knitting, gardening, home/auto projects.)
- Get a massage. Aim for at least one per month.
- Travel. Visit someplace intriguing and new, or familiar and relaxing. Or both.
- Go to a spa for a thorough pampering.
- Keep a journal. Write down when you're feeling stressed, get it all out. Develop solutions if you can, or just allow yourself to relieve the pressure through writing.
- Talk things out with a friend, confidante, mentor, family member, spiritual advisor, or therapist.

Take these words of advice from Trish O'Keefe, President of Morristown Memorial Medical Center:

> Even taking a walk outside makes a difference. It helps to just take a breath, because it is always full speed ahead. Work is all-encompassing and you need some downtime. Getting away recharges me and I promote it for my directors as well. We all need it.

CHAPTER 7

Hitting the Gas

Your Accelerating Success Action Plan

Today's most successful leaders are reflective, strategic, and deliberate in their approach. They don't rush to decisions. They do not act in haste. They pause to review the events and decisions that have gotten them (and their businesses) to the current state. They build upon past success and actively avoid repetitive mistakes. They look out at the horizon. And they thoughtfully carve the path from present to future.

Once you've taken the time to clearly identify your top goals and crystallize your vision, you're ready to develop the plan. Use the exercises throughout the book as your foundation, along with these additional reflection prompts:

- *Where do I want to be, and what do I want to achieve, ins6 months, 1 year, 5, or 10?*

- *What is my vision for the team, department, or business?*
  - ✓ *How will we perform?*
  - ✓ *Where will we rank among the competition?*
  - ✓ *What sort of growth must we achieve?*
  - ✓ *How can we innovate to meet (or create) future market need?*
  - ✓ *How will we differentiate ourselves?*
  - ✓ *Where can we leverage organizational strengths and marketplace opportunities?*

- *Why are these my (our) top goals?*
  - ✓ *How will these goals create success for me, my team, the company?*
  - ✓ *Am I focusing on the right things?*
  - ✓ *Will they bring me a sense of meaning and purpose?*
  - ✓ *Will they make me more fulfilled and content?*
  - ✓ *What's at stake if I (we) don't achieve these goals? What's the cost of doing nothing?*

- *What are the most relevant and impactful actions I (we) can take to quickly progress in achieving these goals?*
  - ✓ *Where and how should I spend my time?*
  - ✓ *With whom must I align, develop trust, communicate, collaborate?*
  - ✓ *How can I build upon past successes and strengths to accelerate progress?*

- *What are the obstacles to success and how can I avoid or overcome them?*
  - ✓ *Who or what may stand in the way of reaching my goals?*
  - ✓ *What are the preventive or corrective actions to clear the hurdles?*
  - ✓ *How can I (we) avoid regrettable repetitions of past mistakes?*
  - ✓ *What lessons can I (we) apply from past failures to accelerate of progress?*

- *How will I recognize success?*
  - ✓ *What are the tangible and intangible indicators of progress?*
  - ✓ *Who are the right people to provide support, encouragement, feedback, and accountability?*

- *How will I implement the plan and achieve rapid gains?*
  - ✓ *What are the timelines for achieving key milestones and attaining long-term success?*
  - ✓ *What can I accomplish quickly, to create momentum?*
  - ✓ *Which actions will be short term? Which take longer to execute?*
  - ✓ *Which actions or behaviors should continue indefinitely?*

Review your responses and use them to craft your plan. Select one to three goals at a time. As you meet with success, you can focus on new goals to support your long-term vision.

And remember, this is an *action* plan. Print out your plan and keep it where you can see it. Review it daily and put it to use.

Use your plan as a reminder to focus on what's most important. Bring it to alignment discussions with your manager, colleagues and team. Have your direct reports create their own action plans, emphasizing business impact, leadership, and career path. Use your ASAP to crystallize business objectives alongside your personal and professional goals. Update and revise your plan regularly to address new challenges and opportunities and reflect changing objectives.

Accelerating Success Action Plan (ASAP)

My Vision:

_____

My Goals:

_____

Goal: *What do I want to achieve? Why is this important? What is at stake?*

Actions: *Which specific actions will help me achieve this goal quickly, effectively and with lasting impact? How will I address challenges and obstacles?*

Resources: *Who/what will help me achieve my goal? How will I secure the help I need?*

Metrics and Timelines: *How will I track progress? What are the milestones? When will I hit milestones? How will I recognize success? When do I expect to achieve this goal?*

Goal:	Actions:	Resources:	Metrics and timelines:

Be sure to track your efforts, record your successes, and develop solutions to challenges that emerge along the way.

CHAPTER 8

In this chapter, you will find worksheets and expanded versions of the lists and tools provided throughout the book. But first, take the following diagnostic survey. Use it to assess whether, and how urgently, you need to slow down. You can use this tool for self-assessment and you can easily adapt it for use with your team and entire organization.

Check Your Speedometer: A Diagnostic Tool

Rate each statement from 1 to 5.

    1 = *Strongly Disagree (or Never)*
    3 = *Somewhat Agree (or Sometimes)*
    5 = *Strongly Agree (or Always)*

1. I set goals for the next month, quarter, and year (not just a daily to-do list). _____
2. I have confidence that my team takes a proactive approach. _____
3. I learn from mistakes and avoid repeating them. _____
4. I can easily identify the people with the greatest influence on my success. _____
5. I prioritize spending time with my key stakeholders. _____
6. I make decisions deliberately and thoughtfully (not by default). _____
7. I use past experiences to inform how I work in the present. _____
8. I review my goals, aspirations, and vision on a regular basis. _____
9. I can readily state my top priorities. _____
10. I quickly delineate whether a task should be handled personally or delegated. _____
11. I feel in control of my inbox; email is a tool, not an unavoidable burden. _____
12. I get adequate and restful sleep. _____

13. I eat a nutritious diet. _____

14. I can carve out time to catch my breath and think strategically during my work day. _____

15. I fully leverage my top skills and talents. _____

Total Score _____

Interpreting Your Results

55 to 75 You're moving at the perfect pace.

Impressive! You are moving at the ideal speed and efficiency for stellar results and sustained success. You're positioned to thrive. You are doing the right things and making strategic decisions. Take time to teach others on your team and across the organization.

45 to 54 Ease off the gas pedal.

You're well on your way to a solid command of the approach needed for greater impact and sustainable success. Pay attention to items with a score of 1 or 2. These are the places where you will benefit most from careful application of the tools in this book. Be sure to implement them deliberately and consistently. You will soon reap the benefits. So will your team, business partners, customers, and entire organization.

5 to 44 Slow down before you crash!

You're in need of a speed intervention before you suffer a head-on collision. You've got to hit the brakes, take a deep breath, and start actively implementing the tools laid out in this book. It's not too late to slow down to speed up!

Strategic Pause Tips

Use the worksheet on the following page to help you get the most from your strategic pauses.

What are my top priorities for the day? The week? The month, quarter, or year?

_____

_____

_____

What must I absolutely accomplish today? What's my plan to get it done?

_____

_____

_____

Which activities can I delegate, delay, or dismiss altogether?

_____

_____

_____

How will I resolve an unpleasant conflict with my boss, peer, or customer?

_____

_____

_____

What was today's greatest success?

_____

_____

_____

How can I build on that success—tomorrow, next week, in the coming month, quarter, or year?

_____

_____

_____

What could I have done differently and how will I apply what I've learned?

_____

_____

_____

Pivot Points: Pivotal Successes/Pivotal Regrets

Pivot Point	Impact

Pivotal Successes	Impact
_____	_____
_____	_____
_____	_____
_____	_____
_____	_____
_____	_____

Pivotal Regrets	Impact
_____	_____
_____	_____
_____	_____
_____	_____
_____	_____
_____	_____

What Do You Love, What Do You Bring, and Where Are You Headed?

What do I value most?

_____

_____

_____

What do I love to do?

_____

_____

_____

What do I bring?

_____

_____

_____

What's holding me back? And how can I fill in the gaps, address blind spots, etc.?

_____

_____

_____

Setting Your Sights: Crafting the Vision and Getting from Here to There

As you develop your vision of a remarkably successful future, take your time to reflect and answer the following:

- *What are you doing, thinking and feeling in this vision?*
- *What accounts for your increased success, confidence, and satisfaction?*
- *How have you improved your approach to leadership or the achievement of your goals?*

- *How does your future self make outstanding decisions, drive strategy, take meaningful action, or develop a new generation of leaders?*
- *What's your future team doing especially well?*
- *How has your company transformed the competitive landscape?*

My Vision

Priority Assessment Tool

1. *Does this activity align with my strategy?* _____
2. *Does this activity directly advance my top goals?* _____
3. *Does my manager/client/colleague agree that it is a top priority item?* _____
4. *Does this activity add significant value?* _____
5. *How pressing is the deadline?* _____

Scoring:

1 = no/not at all

3 = somewhat

5 = yes/very

- An activity receiving a score of 4 or 5 on *three to five* of the above questions is a *top* priority.
- An activity receiving a score of 4 or 5 on *one or two* of the above questions is a priority.
- Everything else is subordinate and should be treated accordingly. You may choose to delay action, delegate to someone else, or take it off your radar entirely.

My top 3 priorities:

1. _____

2. _____

3. _____

CIA: Control, Influence, Accept/Adapt Framework

It's a straightforward framework for making decisions—quickly, efficiently, and without undue stress or wasted energy. The next time you are faced with an important decision, ask yourself:

- *Is this a situation or decision over which I have direct control? If so, how will I exert that control and what outcome do I want to achieve?*

  _____

  _____

  _____

- *If I don't have direct control, can I influence the decision or outcome? If so, how can I most effectively exert that influence?*

  _____

  _____

  _____

- *If I have neither control nor influence, can I accept the situation? It may not be my preference but it's the reality. What can I do, in that case, to make it more palatable, comfortable, positive, and successful? What must I do to adapt? And if I can't accept or adapt . . . what then?*

  _____

  _____

  _____

Stakeholder Priority Plan

Here's a model you can use to categorize your key stakeholders. Keep it close at hand, and modify as structure, roles, challenges, and objectives change over time. Remember, your relationships will have a tremendous impact on your level of success.

Your Plan

Once you've assigned a category to each stakeholder, you'll need to develop a plan to engage them. Consider:

- *Where, when, and how often will you meet?*

  _____

- *How formal or informal, scheduled or ad hoc?*

  _____

- *Will they be 1:1, in small groups, at a Town Hall?*

  _____

- *How quickly must you arrange time to meet?*

  _____

- *How can you build upon the strength of the existing relationship?*

  _____

- *Are there problems that must be fixed?*

  _____

- *What has to happen to rapidly create trust, improve communication, address conflict, or accelerate collaboration?*

  _____

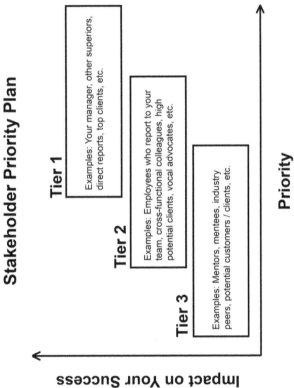

Stakeholder Priority Plan

Tier 1
Examples: Your manager, other superiors, direct reports, top clients, etc.

Tier 2
Examples: Employees who report to your team, cross-functional colleagues, high potential clients, vocal advocates, etc.

Tier 3
Examples: Mentors, mentees, industry peers, potential customers / clients, etc.

Priority

Impact on Your Success

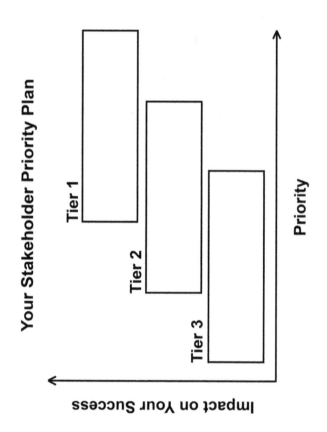

Accelerating Success Action Plan (ASAP)

My Vision:

_____

My Goals:

_____

Goal: *What do I want to achieve? Why is this important? What is at stake?*

Actions: *Which specific actions will help me achieve this goal quickly, effectively and with lasting impact? How will I address challenges and obstacles?*

Resources: *Who/what will help me achieve my goal? How will I secure the help I need?*

Metrics and Timelines: *How will I track progress? What are the milestones? When will I hit milestones? How will I recognize success? When do I expect to achieve this goal?*

Goal:	Actions:	Resources:	Metrics and Timelines:

36 Actions to Accelerate Success

When you take a pause in the busyness of your day, you free up time for a wide variety of actions to help you get better, faster, more sustainable results. Here are 36 ways you can leverage these deliberate breaks in the action.

Assess

1. *Your current situation, challenge, or opportunity.* Examine it from a variety of angles. Is this a near-term priority? Will it help you advance your strategic objectives? When and how will you approach it for the greatest impact and advantage?

2. *The competition.* In which ways does the competition have an advantage? What are your competitor's gaps or weaknesses? How can you differentiate and elevate yourself to gain advantage and increase market share?

3. *Your team.* Look closely at talent, individual and collective performance, potential, behavior, collaboration, communication, conflict resolution, and trust. Is your team performing at the highest possible level? Do you have the right people in the right roles doing the right things? Do you need to make any changes to structure or staffing to accelerate impact and improve outcomes?

4. *Your personal brand, reputation, and credibility within the organization.* Have you earned the respect and recognition of colleagues, managers, and partners? Do others see you as you see yourself? How will you build upon the good and address shortcomings to build a stellar personal brand?

5. *Your reputation with customers and clients.* How are you perceived beyond your organization? Are your customer relationships as strong as they need to be? Are there concerns or problems to be addressed? How can you leverage, change, or improve your reputation?

Align

6. *With your boss.* What are the parameters and primary objectives of your role? What are the key success factors and how will you recognize progress? What is the scope of responsibility and decision-making

authority? How often will you meet? What kind of information must get escalated immediately? How much funding is available to implement your initiatives? What is your career path and what are your most important next steps?

7. *With other stakeholders and business partners.* Ensure mutual understanding and agreement: What are you trying to achieve? What's the strategy? What are the top priorities? What's a reasonable time frame for reaching milestones? How will you collaborate and communicate?

Acknowledge

8. *The contributions of others.* A few words of genuine appreciation can have a tremendous impact. Observe and recognize the efforts and accomplishments of your team and other contributors. Don't hold back.

9. *Stress.* Especially in demanding times, your team will be feeling the pressure. As a leader, you can reduce their feelings of overwhelm, anxiety, and frustration simply by validating the extra burden your team is carrying.

10. *Unspoken tension or conflict* among the team. If you bury your head in the sand and pretend everything is fine, you will only compound the problem. Acknowledge what's happening. Bring it out into the open where it can be resolved.

Assign

11. *Roles and activities* to the people who are most capable of getting it done quickly and well.

Articulate

12. *Your vision.* What is your compelling view of the future? What will the organization look like and where will you be in a year, or five, or farther into the future? Be sure to convey a captivating and inspirational view of what's possible.

13. *Your strategy.* How will you and the organization get from here to there?

14. *Your enthusiasm.* As a leader, you set the tone. Success requires effort, perseverance, and optimism. Share your positivity and zeal with your team, customers, investors—everyone whose support and engagement is essential to achieving remarkable outcomes.

15. *Your concerns.* I'm not suggesting that you share information that doesn't belong in the public purview. You shouldn't worry your organization or your customers about concerns that you, as a leader, must address privately. But do employ a genuine and open style as you communicate potential obstacles to be tackled. This is the foundation for building trust, identifying solutions, and getting past the immediate challenge.

16. *Context.* Your employees will be more engaged, and you will encounter less resistance, when you share the big picture and explain the reasons behind a given approach or change in direction.

Acquire

17. *The support* you will need to achieve your goals. Whose championship and commitment is most needed? Spend time with those people and explain your approach. Show them how helping you brings value to them and the organization.

18. *The resources* you need to expedite progress. Do you need funding? Headcount? Training for the team? Advisors, coaches, or contractors? By proactively lining up the right resources, you will reach your goals much faster.

19. *The knowledge, experience, or advice* needed to advance your career, increase impact, and get to the next level of success.

Address

20. *Concerns.* Don't attempt to ignore or dismiss others' concerns—or your own. Get out in front of the worries. Discuss, address, and remedy them now to avoid trouble down the road.

21. *Questions.* By directly and proactively addressing questions—about decisions, strategy, context, management changes, market challenges, and more—you create clarity. And clarity will help you accelerate progress, avoid mistakes, and prevent unwanted disruptions. It takes time, but the return on that time will be exponential.

22. *Obstacles.* A leader cannot afford to bury his or her head in the sand. There will always be obstacles to progress. The sooner and more thoughtfully you address these challenges, the faster you will get to your goal.

23. *Expectations.* What are others expecting of you, your team, or a given initiative? Don't wait for people to come to you. Take the lead. Address expectations and revisit them over time. Ask your stakeholders: *Am I (are we) meeting your expectations? What's working well and what needs to be revised?*

Assist

24. *Your colleagues, manager, team members, customers, and clients.* By taking the time to lend a hand—by going out of your way to be there for the people who need and rely upon you—you establish yourself as a leader who cares. You build strong relationships. You increase trust. All these are essential for impactful leadership.

Ask

25. *How others are faring in the face of challenge and change.* Check in with colleagues, employees, business partners, and customers. When you make a personal connection, you build trust, strengthen relationships, and foster open communication.

26. *Pertinent questions.* There is no prize for being clairvoyant. Don't try to read the minds of people around you and don't wing it when information is unclear or lacking. Ask relevant, thought-provoking questions to ensure complete understanding and open the door to meaningful discussion.

27. *For help.* Many leaders are reluctant to ask for help, out of concern that they will appear weak. The truth is it takes courage to be vulnerable. Ask for the help you need. You'll be setting a great example for the people around you.

28. *For specificity and context.* If you're only getting the gestalt, you probably need to request additional information. This will help you understand expectations and clarify your role in achieving a goal.

29. *For dissenting and divergent points of view.* Even if you are the ultimate decision maker, you should engage others in the process by soliciting ideas and perspectives. Where are the potential challenges or obstacles you might otherwise miss? Is there a better way? Give others an opportunity to share how they see a given situation, and your decision will be better informed as a result. By seeking input from others, you'll also increase the buy-in and trust of those who would resist a dictatorial approach.

Anticipate

30. *Changing conditions.* Don't let changes in the marketplace, regulatory environment, talent pool, or global economy take you by surprise. Look around and ahead to anticipate, adapt, and leverage changing conditions.

31. *Resistance.* When you propose something new, you will encounter resistance. Expect it. Be ready to address it head-on to mitigate the drag it can create.

32. *Opportunities.* For yourself, your team, and your company. When you see opportunity before it arrives, you set yourself up for success. Anticipate what's coming down the pike so you can fully leverage it. In the famous words of Louis Pasteur, "Fortune favors the prepared mind."

33. *Questions.* Which questions or concerns are likely to emerge regarding a given project, strategy, or decision? Take the time to think them through. If you anticipate the questions likely to come your way, you can prepare thoughtful and convincing responses.

Accentuate

34. *Behavior.* Yes, performance matters. But it's not enough to get the work done. Getting it done ethically, responsibly, respectfully, and collaboratively matters just as much. Be sure your team understands and adheres to your behavioral expectations.

35. *What's going well.* By focusing on the positive and emphasizing opportunity, progress and growth, you help your team to remain inspired and motivated even when times get tough.

Advise, Train, and Develop

36. *Your team.* Even the smartest and most dedicated employees require advice, direction, mentoring, and training to do their jobs well. In the words of Jeff Moody, former CEO of Rita's Italian Ice and Subway Franchise Advertising Fund Trust:

> When I was a division VP with Pizza Hut we had a training principle that transcends any single brand: When you train an employee on a new product and have them make it three times properly, the process gets ingrained. They'll make it properly forever. If you don't supervise them, it is almost impossible to get them to learn the right procedure. Taking the time to properly train is critical.

Index

Accelerating success action plan (ASAP), 46, 73–76, 89

Control, influence, accept/adapt (CIA) framework, 53–56, 85

Decision making, 6–7
  estimation of, 7
  hasty, 8–10
  in hiring employees, 9
  lack of communication, 7
  problem in, 6, 9
  responding to e-mail, 7
Decisiveness, 3

Leadership, 3
  going too fast, 3–4
  hasty decisions, 8–10
  impact of slowing down, 12–13
  making mistakes, 4
  moving too fast, 5–6
  number of decisions, making, 6–7
  rapid hiring, 9
  real problem of e-mail, 8
  regrettable repetitions, 10–12
  responsibility of, 3
  responsive to clients, 4
  stamina for, 67–68
  strategic pause, 15–21

Pivotal regrets, 31–35, 41, 81
Pivotal successes, 28–31, 81
Pivot points, 25–27
  asking yourself, 27
  considerations, 26
  to reflect on business challenge, 26
  template for, 27
  worksheet for, 80
Priority assessment tool, 53, 84

Regrettable repetitions, 10–12

Self-reflection, 25
Slowing down
  actions to accelerate success, 22–23, 91–96
  accentuate, 95
  acknowledge, 92
  acquire, 93
  address, 93–94
  advise, 96
  align, 91–92
  anticipate, 95
  articulate, 92–93
  ask, 94–95
  assess, 91
  assign, 92
  assist, 94
  develop, 96
  train, 96
  adjusting approach, 43–44
  anticipating obstacles, 11
  considering approach, 11
  assessing organization, 37–38
  bringing the good, 39–41, 82
  developing vision, 45–47, 82–83
  impact of, 12–13
  importance of, 10
  leadership challenge, facing, 41
  learning from past, 4
  other ways to, 15–21
  pivotal regrets, 31–35
  pivotal successes, 28–31
  pivot points and reflections, 25–27
  to reflect on goals, 12
  reflect on hurdles in way, 41–42
  seeking opportunities, 40
  sharing success stories, 12
  strategic pause, 15–21
  striking balance, 21–22
  thoughtful path, developing, 11

Speeding up
    control, influence, accept/adapt
        (CIA) framework, 53–56
    diplomatically defer, decline, or
        deflect, 60
    direct responsibilities, 57–58
    eating well, 70
    minimizing stress, 71
    "now/later/never" in doing tasks,
        59–60
    prioritization challenge, mastering,
        51–53
    priority assessment tool, 53
    putting oxygen mask, 68–69
    relax, recharge, refuel, 67–71
    sleeping well, 70
    stakeholder priority plan (SPP),
        63–68
    "start saying no!" to clients, 56–57
    targeted e-mail response system
        (TERS), 60–63
Stakeholder priority plan (SPP), 13,
    63–68, 86–88
Strategic pause, 15–21
    definition of, 15
    for effective leadership, 16–17
    importance of, 17
    time to calm yourself, 18
    use of, 17
    worksheet for, 79–80

Targeted e-mail response system
    (TERS), 60–63
Tier one stakeholders, 64
Tier three stakeholders, 64
Tier two stakeholders, 64

OTHER TITLES IN THE HUMAN RESOURCE MANAGEMENT AND ORGANIZATIONAL BEHAVIOR COLLECTION

- *The Illusion of Inclusion: Global Inclusion, Unconscious Bias, and the Bottom Line* by Helen Turnbull
- *On All Cylinders: The Entrepreneur's Handbook* by Ron Robinson
- *Employee LEAPS: Leveraging Engagement by Applying Positive Strategies* by Kevin E. Phillips
- *Making Human Resource Technology Decisions: A Strategic Perspective* by Janet H. Marler and Sandra L. Fisher
- *Feet to the Fire: How to Exemplify And Create The Accountability That CreatesGreat Companies* by Lorraine A. Moore
- *HR Analytics and Innovations in Workforce Planning* by Tony Miller
- *Deconstructing Management Maxims, Volume I: A Critical Examination of Conventional Business Wisdom* by Kevin Wayne
- *Deconstructing Management Maxims, Volume II: A Critical Examination of Conventional Business Wisdom* by Kevin Wayne
- *The Real Me: Find and Express Your Authentic Self* by Mark Eyre
- *Across the Spectrum: What Color Are You?* by Stephen Elkins-Jarrett
- *Life of a Lifetime: Inspiration for Creating Your Extraordinary Life* by Christoph Spiessens
- *The Facilitative Leader: Managing Performance Without Controlling People* by Steve Reilly
- *The Human Resource Professional's Guide to Change Management: Practical Tools and Techniques to Enact Meaningful and Lasting Organizational Change* by Melanie J. Peacock
- *Tough Calls: How to Move Beyond Indecision and Good Intentions* by Linda D. Henman
- *Human Resources as Business Partner: How to Maximize The Value and Financial Contribution of HR* by Tony Miller

Announcing the Business Expert Press Digital Library

Concise e-books business students need for classroom and research

This book can also be purchased in an e-book collection by your library as

- *a one-time purchase,*
- *that is owned forever,*
- *allows for simultaneous readers,*
- *has no restrictions on printing, and*
- *can be downloaded as PDFs from within the library community.*

Our digital library collections are a great solution to beat the rising cost of textbooks. E-books can be loaded into their course management systems or onto students' e-book readers.
The **Business Expert Press** digital libraries are very affordable, with no obligation to buy in future years. For more information, please visit **www.businessexpertpress.com/librarians**. To set up a trial in the United States, please email **sales@businessexpertpress.com**.

CPSIA information can be obtained
at www.ICGtesting.com
Printed in the USA
FSHW021837210220